# HOW TO SURVIVE THE RECESSION OF 1991

Y0-DDS-195

- Easy and painless ways to save
- Where to put your money and when
- Losing your job and finding a new one
- Credit, debt, and the cash crunch
- Coping emotionally and psychologically
- Financing a new home, paying college tuition, and starting a new business
- Entertainment, dining, and fashion on a budget

PLUS: Worksheets and charts . . . Money action tips . . . Lists of high-yield stocks and investments . . . Useful publications, address-es, and telephone numbers . . . Glossaries of financial and recession terms . . . AND MORE!

## EVERYTHING YOU NEED TO KNOW TO TRIUMPH OVER ECONOMIC ADVERSITY!

NANCY DUNNAN is a financial columnist for *Lear's* magazine and is the author of numerous financial books, including *How to Invest $50-$5000* and *Dun & Bradstreet Guide to Your Investments*.

JAY J. PACK is a stockbroker, certified financial planner, and the author of *How to Talk to a Broker*.

# HOW TO SURVIVE & THRIVE IN THE RECESSION OF 1991

**NANCY DUNNAN & JAY J. PACK**

AVON BOOKS ◆ NEW YORK

This book offers only general financial advice. The authors have attempted to ensure that all information in this book is accurate. However, errors can occur, some rules and regulations may vary from area to area, from bank to bank . . . In addition, interest rates and stock prices change daily. Therefore, the authors and the publisher disclaim responsibility for the complete accuracy of the text. And as is always mere common sense, the reader is cautioned to consult a qualified accountant or attorney regarding accounting or legal problems.

HOW TO SURVIVE & THRIVE IN THE RECESSION OF 1991 is an original publication of Avon Books. This work has never before appeared in book form.

AVON BOOKS
A division of
The Hearst Corporation
105 Madison Avenue
New York, New York 10016

First Avon Books Printing: April 1991

AVON TRADEMARK REG. U.S. PAT. OFF. AND IN OTHER COUNTRIES, MARCA REGIS-
TRADA, HECHO EN U.S.A.

Printed in the U.S.A.

RA   10   9   8   7   6   5   4   3   2   1

The authors wish to thank the following people who
contributed their valuable time and expertise:

Flaherty Research Associates
Christine Kinser, publisher of Cloverdale Press
Marcy Ross, researcher

# Contents

**Introduction**     1

**Chapter 1:**    From Boom to Bust—
And Somewhere In Between    2

**Chapter 2:**    Where to Put Your Money
and When    27

**Chapter 3:**    Spotting Industries
that Will Thrive    58

**Chapter 4:**    Losing Your Job and
Finding a New One    73

**Chapter 5:**    Credit, Debt, and the
Cash Crunch    118

**Chapter 6:**    The Energy Crunch    148

**Chapter 7:**    It's Chic to Be Cheap    163

**Epilogue**     189

**Index**     191

# Introduction

*"Dare you make war on war. Here are the means."*
George Bernard Shaw
*Act III*, Major Barbara

WE say, "Dare you make war on recession." This book provides the means. Some of these means may be familiar but neglected concepts—like saving money on a regular basis. Others will be brand new. All of them are sound ideas that you can put to good use at any time.

If you're buying a house, sending a child to college, starting a family, considering new investments, or embarking on a number of other financial turning points, you will find the advice given here applies at any time in the economic cycle.

But right now we are all seriously affected by the recession. Each chapter of this book is devoted to reducing that impact, whether you are married, single, a parent, running your own business, out of work, or doing fine but hoping to do better.

If you are worried about your finances—and just about everyone is—or even feeling frightened, don't panic. Let the dust settle and a little time go by as you read this book. Surviving and thriving in a recession is a matter of getting the best information: Here it is.

1

# From Boom to Bust—and Somewhere In Between

RECESSION. You've been hearing that word for some time. And by now, it has probably started to affect your life. You may not be able to sell your house; you may not be getting a raise or bonus this year; you may be out of work or worried that you soon will be. Even if you don't have any of these concerns, the gloomy news has no doubt affected your feelings about business, finance, and your family's prosperity in the days ahead. And it's all due to the "R" word. What is it? How long will it last? What will it mean to you? Without a crystal ball we can't answer the last two questions. But we can explain the first—what is it?

## A RECESSION BY ANY OTHER NAME

Officially, the term recession is applied when the gross national product (GNP), the total value of all goods and services produced and sold in the United States, declines for two consecutive quarters. As of January 1991, that has not happened yet. *Yet.* Anyone who reads the papers or listens to the news knows that the "R" word is already being applied to our current economy. Most economists say that this recession actually began in the summer of 1990. By December of 1990 the leading economic indicators had dropped for the fifth straight month. Although Federal Reserve chairman Alan Greenspan labeled it a "meaningful downturn" in late November 1990, there are only a handful of experts refusing to admit we're in the midst of a recession. But back to our original question: What is a recession?

It is a natural—and expected—part of the U.S. business cycle. This up-and-down pattern of economic activity has been surging from boom to bust for more than 100 years. The business cycle, which generally runs three to four years from beginning to end, starts when interest rates and inflation are low. At this point it's easy for consumers to borrow money and to buy homes, cars, boats, and other large-ticket items. There's even enough money left over for jewelry, vacations, art, and antiques. Corporations borrow, too, as they rush to increase production. Investors, seeing or expecting higher corporate profits, buy stocks and the Dow Jones heads up. Business is good and nearly every part of the economy grows. Jobs are plentiful and employment is high.

It's too much of a good thing. As demand for credit increases, interest rates start to rise as more and more borrowers compete for loans. At the same time, more goods are purchased sometimes causing higher inflation. The rising demand for manufactured goods allows manufacturers to raise their prices, resulting in inflation which is also due to the increase in the cost of labor. (Inflation is also caused by rising oil prices.) Real estate prices escalate as more prospective buyers have access to mortgages.

Suddenly, there's too much consumer debt and houses are too high in price to move. People no longer want to borrow. Interest rates are high enough to send stock prices down, and to put a crimp on spending and borrowing. The expansionary phase of the business cycle draws to a close. This inevitable slowdown occurs at some point in every expansion when consumers realize they can no longer handle additional debt.

Businesses then see that demand for their products and services are no longer on the rise and so they, too, cut back, reducing production and lowering prices in order to move merchandise off their shelves and out of their warehouses. As soon as both consumer and business borrowing and spending decline, production and income fall and a contraction begins. People are laid off and unemployment rises. The economy literally recedes. If it's severe enough and lasts long enough, it's labeled a recession.

## A THUMBNAIL SKETCH OF
## PREVIOUS RECESSIONS

This is by no means the country's first recession. As of 1989, the U.S. has had seven recessions since the end of World War II. Each time, the GNP fell and unemployment rose. The good news is that on the average a recession only lasts a year.

- *1948–1949*. The postwar boom ended with this eleven-month slump. GNP fell 2%; unemployment reached 7.9%.
- *1953–1954*. After the Korean War, defense spending fell and the GNP dropped 2.6%; unemployment reached 5.9%.
- *1957–1958*. During this slowdown, the GNP fell 3.5%.
- *1960–1961*. The GNP fell 1% and unemployment hit 6.9%.
- *1969–1970*. A mild decline, largely due to a General Motors strike. The GNP fell 0.08%.
- *1973–1975*. This was the longest and toughest recession since World War II, with oil prices quadrupling. The GNP fell 4.3% and unemployment soared from 4.9% to 8.5%.
- *1981–1982*. The Fed set off this recession when it fought double-digit inflation by letting interest rates reach 20%. The GNP fell 3.4% and unemployment hit 10.8%.

All these recessions share one positive characteristic—they came to an end. And so will this one. Whereas an expansion typically peaks when consumers are no longer willing to borrow and spend, a recession ends when consumer confidence returns. Yet, until this particular recession self-corrects, we suggest you use the advice given in the following chapters. Much of it applies to non-recessionary times as well so that the ideas offered in this book will make you a more savvy manager of your personal, professional, and financial life. Pay particular attention to the *$$ ACTION TIPS*—these are simple steps you can take right now to shore up your finances and ride out the recession in comfort, if not in style.

## UNDERSTANDING RECESSION-SPEAK

As you listen to the news or flip through the newspaper, you're bound to encounter a lot of jargon. The government spews it out faster than Daryll Strawberry hits home runs. Although these words and statistics may seem irrelevant to your everyday life, they are in fact very much a part of it. By learning how to interpret the lingo, you will know what's happening to the economy and your place within it, and you will gain advance warning of what's taking place. It can help you make a number of decisions about your savings, expenditures, and investments. Subsequent chapters will examine these areas in depth, but first let's take a look at how you can keep abreast of the current situation through the media.

To start, you need to know the eleven most popular terms which describe an aspect of the business cycle. (The meanings of additional economic terms are explained in the appendix.) Understanding these terms won't transform you into a professional economist, but they will show you how to find and interpret economic data in order to make intelligent personal and business decisions.

- Capacity Utilization (Factory Operating Rate)

   This statistic (actually a percentage) measures the activity of U.S. manufacturers. Full capacity would be 100%, although that's not truly obtainable. Usually, 85% is optimal, and even a few percentage points higher strains our industrial system. Capacity utilization drops to a comfortable and more efficient level during a recession. It's rather like a car, which operates more efficiently at 55 mph than at 70 mph. *What it means to you:* When capacity utilization is low, unemployment is high.

- Consumer Price Index (CPI)

   The CPI, also known as the cost of living index, is a broad measure of price changes for goods and services. Among the CPI components are: costs of housing, food, transportation, clothing, medical care and electricity.

### Consumer Price Index 1988–1990
Year-to-year percent change

(Source: U.S. Department of Labor)

*What it means to you:* If the CPI rises by only 2% a year, inflation is low; 2–4% is moderate; above 4% is relatively high and worrisome. However, when this rate rises above 7–8%, inflation is out of sight and your cost of living will go up as well. When the CPI rises, it also has a negative impact on stocks, bonds, and CDs. For example, if you bought a four-year $1,000 Treasury note or CD yielding 8% annually, you would receive $80 a year in interest. But if consumer prices are leaping ahead by 5%, the real purchasing power of your $80 in interest is declining by 5% a year.

• Consumer Sentiment

This index, based on a poll of how consumers feel about spending money, is one of the most closely followed economic indicators. Consumer sentiment is low at the bottom of the business cycle and becomes increasingly optimistic as the economy expands. *What it means to you:* A drop in consumer sentiment is a clear warning that a recession is on its way.

• Gross National Product (GNP)

The GNP measures the total value of all goods and services produced and sold in the U.S. economy over a particular time period, such as one year or one quarter. It tells us whether the economy is expanding or contracting. Less than 2% is regarded as slow growth; 2–5% is respectable and above 5% is a boom, and usually an unsustainable boom. When the GNP figures are adjusted for inflation— that is, when any increase in prices is subtracted from the results— the figure is called real or constant-dollar GNP. The GNP includes consumer and government purchases, private domestic and foreign investments in the U.S., and the total value of exports. *What it means to you:* When the GNP declines two quarters in a row, it indicates that a recession has begun.

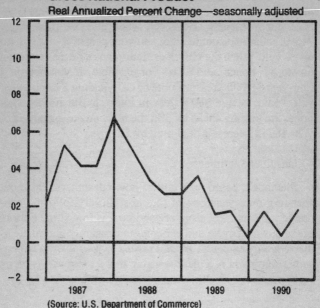

**Gross National Product**
Real Annualized Percent Change—seasonally adjusted

(Source: U.S. Department of Commerce)

• Housing Starts

The Commerce Department reports the number of houses and apartment units on which work has begun each month. This figure is closely watched as an indicator of consumer confidence in the economy. Housing starts are sensitive to mortgage rates: When mortgage rates rise, credit is both expensive and tight, and so housing starts decline. *What it means to you:* When housing starts drop we may be headed into a recession and real estate prices will fall, making it a good time for those who can afford it, to buy.

• Index of Leading Economic Indicators

The index represents an average of eleven components of economic growth, ranging from stock prices to housing permits. *What it means to you:* This is a useful peek at the near future. If the index falls for three or four consecutive months, there could be a setback soon and a recession within the year.

**Leading Economic Indicators 1988–1990**
In percent; 1982 = 100

(Source: U.S. Department of Commerce)

- Interest Rates

Interest rates affect the cost of borrowing money as well as the rate you will earn on your cash, CDs, and money market fund. Interest rates are constantly changing. In an expanding economy, consumers and corporations borrow money; consequently interest rates rise because money is in high demand. In a recession, however, demand for borrowed money declines and interest rates, too, decline. To find out the direction in which interest rates are moving, check the "Credit Markets" column in the *New York Times* or similar material in other newspapers or magazines. Look for the prime rate, the rate banks charge their top customers for loans. When the prime goes up it means that corporations are borrowing and the economy is expanding. Consumer loans are pegged to prime, so use this as a barometer to your own loan rates. Also follow the three-month Treasury bill yields. When yields rise it may mean a return of inflation and eventually a slowdown in the economy. *What it means to you:* When interest rates rise you want to be invested in bonds, CDs, and money market funds; when rates fall, move into stocks, real estate, and tangibles.

- Producer Price Index (PPI)

This index shows changes in the wholesale prices charged by producers of all *finished* goods, in other words, all manufactured goods. When the U.S. economy starts to expand vigorously, producers raise their prices and this index also rises. The consumer equivalent of this index is the CPI. *What it means to you:* When this index starts to rise, expect to pay more for U.S.-manufactured goods.

- Retail Sales

This dollar figure includes everything sold by retailers, from automobiles to gasoline to sales made by department and specialty stores. Retail sales are usually on the rise because Americans are robust consumers. Only in periods of tight credit or severe recessions do retail sales drop off. *What it means to you:* If retail sales drop dramatically it may indicate a severe recession.

- Standard & Poor's 500 Index (S&P 500)

For many economists and stock market professionals, the Dow Jones Industrial Average, based on the price movements of the stocks of only thirty companies, is too narrow to be a reliable indicator of the market. So they also follow the S&P 500, an index of the price movement of 500 corporations in all areas of the economy. *What it means to you:* Stock market behavior sometimes gives advance notice of the direction of the economy because investors buy stocks based on their feelings about the future. The market may be excessively nervous. It's an old Wall Street joke that the stock market has predicted nine out of the last five recessions! But the S&P still remains a solid measure of its future. When the S&P 500 starts to rise, expansion lies ahead for the economy. However, when it drops significantly, watch for a recession.

• Unemployment

The Department of Labor releases the number of unemployed, as a percent of the total labor force, each month. An unemployment rate of 6% or less is considered moderate;

**Unemployment Rate 1988–1990**
Percent of labor force, seasonally adjusted

(Source: U.S. Department of Labor)

4–5% is regarded almost as full employment. During the 1983 recession unemployment hovered around 10%. *What it means to you:* Rising unemployment is a key indicator of a recession. When the unemployment figure stops rising and levels off, we have reached the bottom of the recession.

## THE BEST IN MEDIA COVERAGE

Now that you understand the major series of economic statistics and what the changes in these figures imply for the future of the business cycle, you're all set to read or listen to the financial news. Even though you might have grown up feeling that financial matters were beyond you, by devoting an hour or hour and a half each week to either reading financial material or watching one of the many financial programs you will quickly develop an understanding of what is happening to the economy and your money.

Let's begin with the *Wall Street Journal*. The front page presents each new statistical number in chart form—you can find all of the key indicators that we've discussed in the previous pages, such as GNP, housing starts, etc. These are presented once a month as they become available. On page two of the same section, known as Section A, you will also find interpretations of quarterly or monthly changes in the GNP, capacity utilization, consumer spending, etc., by professional economists. These economists try to determine whether we are in a period of expansion, near the peak, or beginning a contraction. *Business Week* contains equally detailed material on the economic scene. Other magazines and newspapers are listed on page 16.

Another way to learn the opinions of experts is through television—in particular the "Nightly Business Report" on the public broadcasting system (PBS), "Business Day" and "Moneyline" on Cable News Network (CNN), "Adam Smith's Money World," and, the longest-running financial show, "Wall Street Week." The latter two are also on PBS.

# A CRITIC'S GUIDE TO BROADCAST FINANCE

You may feel that unless you're a financial guru there's very little for you on TV finance shows. Yet neophytes as well as pros find these broadcasts entertaining as well as educational. They can be a painless way to learn how to handle money, where to invest and why. Many programs offer such tangible suggestions as when to switch from stocks to bonds, whether to buy one-year or four-year CDs, whether it's a good time to buy or sell a house, which countries offer the most value for the dollar and where to find the best mortgage rates. So, tune in and keep turning the dial until you find the program that suits you best. The critical guide that follows should give you some ideas as to where to start.

## THE WEEKLY SHOWS

"Adam Smith's Money World"
PBS, Tuesday, 9:30 P.M. EST, ½ hour
*Format:* Interesting graphic presentation of a current business issue followed by a discussion with one or two experts.
*Pros:* Fascinating topics and thorough coverage.
*Cons:* Does not give specific advice.

A thoughtful and perceptive program, hosted by Adam Smith, who takes his name from the eighteenth-century Scottish economist who championed free trade. Each week Smith selects one important financial event and then, using graphics, films, and taped interviews, explains why and how it happened as well as the impact it will have on the American public.

"Wall Street Week with Louis Rukeyser"
PBS, Friday, 8:30 P.M. EST, ½ hour
*Format:* Host and panel discuss the past week's stock market performance and answer questions from viewers during

first half of show. A well-known financial expert talks to the panel and Rukeyser during the second half.

*Pros:* Practical advice given on stocks, bonds, and mutual funds. Popularizes what for many is a dull subject.

*Cons:* The host's attempt to combine wit and wisdom is not always successful. Format has become rigid over the years.

The financial news as entertainment appeals to experts and novices alike. The top-flight Wall Street pros and business experts are often interesting and almost always informative. The primary focus is the stock market whereas Adam Smith's program is more business- and economically oriented.

"The Wall Street Journal Report"
Syndicated to many local stations, Sunday, 11 A.M. EST, ½ hour

*Format:* Editor/anchorperson Consuelo Mack and a team of reporters cover current business and consumer issues.

*Pros:* Covers a variety of current topics.

*Cons:* Is not particularly investment-oriented.

Although not as smooth as the Smith or Rukeyser shows, "The Wall Street Journal Report" covers more consumer subjects, such as banking, senior citizens, new products, and other topics often ignored by TV.

## THE DAILY SHOWS

"The Nightly Business Report"
PBS, Monday through Friday, 6:30 P.M. EST, ½ hour

*Format:* Two anchorpersons and a financial commentator give daily business news plus stock, bond, and commodity prices.

*Pros:* Thorough, wide-ranging coverage.

*Cons:* Not instructive; no specific investment advice.

Due in part to its affiliation with Reuters International

News Service, this show has excellent coverage of overseas financial news as well as intelligent daily summaries of the domestic financial markets.

## THE CABLE NETWORKS

Cable News Network (CNN)

CNN, which broadcasts twenty-four hours a day, seven days a week, covers all types of news, and, of course, includes financial and business topics. Wall Street updates are given every half hour on weekdays. CNN has the largest business news staff in television and it produces various half-hour programs on special financial topics and events.

The weekday financial news begins at 6:30 A.M. EST with "Business Morning" cohosted by Stuart Varney and Deborah Marchini. The same two anchors at 7:30 A.M. EST give more news on "Business Day." On Saturdays, "Moneyweek" at 9:30 A.M. reviews major business and financial developments. "Inside Business" on Sundays at 6:30 P.M. is a one-on-one interview with a business newsmaker. "Your Money" on Saturdays at 3:30 P.M. EST gives consumer tips and personal money advice for individual investors. Wall Street updates are given every hour on the half hour on weekdays.

"Moneyline," CNN's premier program, airs Monday through Friday at 7 P.M. EST and is repeated at 11 P.M. It gives an excellent wrap-up of the financial news and the stock market.

Financial News Network (FNN)

This cable network has continuous coverage of business by station hosts **plus** the constantly updated stock ticker which makes it valuable for serious investors. It offers timely investment advice by the nation's top experts. CAUTION: Watch out for FNN's commercials. Some almost appear like independent advice rather than ads.

## YOUR FINANCIAL DATA BANK

Read or watch one of the following each week.

*Publications* (in order of sophistication, beginning with the most elementary):
  *USA Today*
  Your local newspaper
  *U.S. News & World Report*
  *Money Maker*
  *Money*
  Standard & Poor's *The Outlook*
  *The New York Times*
  *The Wall Street Journal*
  *Business Week*
  *Barron's*
  *Value Line*
  *The Economist*

*TV Financial Shows:*

| | |
|---|---|
| "Business Day" | CNN |
| "The Nightly Business Report" | PBS |
| "Moneyline" | CNN |
| "Adam Smith's Money World" | PBS |
| "Wall Street Week" | PBS |

## YOUR PERSONAL FINANCES

As you read the periodicals or watch the financial programs, you will quickly learn that the first step in taking control over your personal finances is establishing a savings plan. To do this you must create a budget so you know exactly where your money should be going—and where too much of it *is* going! Unless you're lucky enough to win the lottery, budgeting and saving is an inevitable fact of life. It's always important to build substantial savings at any time, but during a recession, it's a real necessity.

In subsequent chapters you'll learn about investment vehicles, credit and debt, cutting everyday expenses, and other aspects of your personal financial plan. But first, let's take a look at savings:

## HOW BIG A NEST EGG DO YOU NEED?

Nearly every financial book says the rule of thumb is to stash three months' worth of living expenses in a money market fund or savings account. Yet, like all such rules, it's not always true. During a recession that figure should be increased to *at least* six months. If you or your spouse lose your job, it may take longer than three months to find a new one.

## SAVINGS TIPS

Ideally you already have a comfortable nest egg, but that's the ideal. Most of us aren't that disciplined. So begin saving today regardless of your income or the amount you can tuck away. Extra money not only makes dreams come true and life a little easier, it also provides some peace of mind should you or your spouse lose your job.

You will find most of these proven ways to save fairly easy, although a few require some belt-tightening. One way to get started is to give yourself a deadline. Resolve to begin a savings program before the end of the week, or at least by the end of this month.

1. *Pay yourself second.* Put aside money before you spend it. Once a month when you pay your bills, write a check to deposit in your money market fund (see page 30 for a list) or savings account at your bank or credit union.

Make the check you write to yourself your second or third check, right after those for the rent or mortgage and utilities. If you wait until after you've paid all your bills, you may never save at all. Aim to save ½ of 1% of your take-home pay the first month; then increase the amount by ½% each month. If you can afford it, double or triple the percentage you sock away.

2. _Use automatic savings plans_. If you don't see it, you won't spend it. Arrange for a certain amount—it can be as little as $50—to be taken out of your paycheck and automatically transferred to your savings or money market account at a bank or credit union. And ask if your employer has an automatic purchase plan for EE savings bonds. Two alternatives are to have your bank automatically transfer a certain amount from checking to savings each month; or have funds automatically withdrawn from your checking account and put in a money market fund.

3. _Leave credit cards at home_. Pay with cash or by check. You will spend less and you'll avoid monthly interest charges on unpaid credit card balances. This approach also helps you "feel" how much you're spending and eliminates impulse purchases.

4. _Defer taxes_. Money in an IRA, Keogh, 401(k), or other qualified retirement plan grows tax-free until withdrawn, ideally when you're retired and in a lower tax bracket. In some of these plans, the employer adds to the employee's contribution. With a 401(k), the money you contribute reduces your taxable income. In most cases, you can fund these plans by making small contributions several times a year rather than trying to pay in one large lump sum. There are other investments that are fully or partially tax-exempt such as municipal bonds, municipal bond mutual funds, EE savings bonds, and U.S. Treasury securities.

5. *Use employee stock option plans*. These offer employees an opportunity to accumulate stock with before-tax dollars. It may be in the form of a stock bonus plan—essentially a profit-sharing plan—or through an ESOP, or employee stock ownership plan. The typical ESOP is a separate entity that borrows to buy shares and distributes stock to each employee. The company then provides the ESOP with the money needed to repay the loan over time. Many companies allow employees to contribute part of their salary to buy the firm's stock through automatic payroll deductions.

6. *Reinvest stock dividends*. Instead of spending dividend checks, automatically have dividends reinvested to buy more of the company's stock. If you own common stock, call the company's shareholder relations division and find out if they offer a DRIP (dividend reinvestment plan) in which existing stockholders can automatically reinvest quarterly dividends in additional shares of the firm's stock. Over 1,000 companies have DRIPs. Many offer new shares at a discount price and sidestep a stockbroker's commission. Some companies, such as McDonald's, Bristol-Meyers, and Clorox, also allow stockholders to make cash purchases of new stocks so that investors can steadily accumulate stock without paying high commissions and without having to buy round lots of 100 shares at a time.

   $$ ACTION TIP: For a complete list of DRIPs, send $4.95 to Dow Theory Forecasts, Inc., 7412 Calumet Avenue, Hammond, IN 46324-2692; 219-931-6480. CAUTION: With some companies you may have to pay a small fee—$5 to $10—when you buy shares. You will also have to pay tax on your dividends even if you reinvest them.

7. *Keep making payments*. When you've paid off a mortgage or a loan, continue to write a check for the same

amount (or at least half the amount) every month and put it into savings. You've learned to live without that money, so now you can sock it away.

8. *Save your change at the end of the day.* Small amounts add up quickly. At the end of the day put your nickels, dimes, and quarters in a jar.

9. *Increase withholding.* By taking fewer deductions than you're entitled to, it's easy to set aside more money than necessary and guarantee yourself a refund when you pay your taxes. If you do not receive a regular salary, you can accomplish the same thing by paying more than the specified amount on quarterly estimated tax installments. There is a disadvantage to this method: The money you save doesn't earn interest, but if you need help saving, use it anyway.

10. *Skip a biggie.* Pick out one very large expense. Then eliminate it or find a cheaper alternative. For example, take one less vacation or cut a trip in half, or work out at the Y instead of at a posh health club.

11. *Pay off credit card charges.* Don't use credit cards as a financing tool. Always pay the balance within thirty days to avoid hefty finance charges.

12. *Set up an envelope system.* Put small amounts of money in separate envelopes to be used for treats or emergencies.

13. *Consolidate high rate debts.* Replace consumer debts on which you may be paying outrageous rates with a home equity loan at a lower rate. (See pages 133–134 for information on home equity loans.) Interest on a home equity loan is deductible on your income tax return.

14. *Don't pay if it's free.* Find no-fee or discounted financial services. Use a discount stockbroker, no-fee checking accounts, and no-load mutual funds. Buy Treasury issues through the mail or your area Federal Reserve bank. Buy savings bonds where you work or at your

local bank. Shop around for the bank with the best checking account deal. No-fee mutual funds include:

| | |
|---|---|
| Fidelity | 800-544-8888 |
| Rushmore | 800-343-3355 |
| Scudder | 800-225-2470 |
| T. Rowe Price | 800-638-5660 |
| Twentieth Century | 800-345-2021 |
| Vanguard | 800-662-7447 |

15. Read Chapter 6, "The Energy Crunch," and Chapter 7, "It's Chic to Be Cheap." You will find that there are many more painless ways to save.

## THE PSYCHOLOGY OF SAVING

Unlike the Japanese, who save as much as 25% or more of their income, the average American puts away only about 5% of his or her pretax earnings. One of the reasons for our bad savings habit is that we try to buy self-esteem through the *things* we purchase. We want to keep up with the Joneses, have our kids in the right schools, join an expensive health club, have new cars and expensive watches. Such spending, or overspending, is encouraged by credit cards.

If you have trouble saving:

- *Keep a log* of where your money goes. For a month, write down everything you spend. You'll see how much you waste on "unnecessaries" such as taxis, magazines, snacks, and other impulse purchases.

- *When you do save*, put it in a nonliquid investment where you can't get at it easily, such as a CD—you'll be penalized if you take it out before it's reached maturity.

- *Treat yourself*. Encourage yourself to save by taking an intermittent treat when you reach a certain goal. Make it a small one (dinner out, a new pair of shoes, a bottle of champagne) so you won't derail your longer, more serious goal of building a nest egg.

## BUDGETS

As you create your savings plan, you should also be making out a budget. Budgeting and savings are closely related. Your first budget will reflect your current expenses. If it doesn't leave you with any money to sock away in savings, then you will have to go back and create a budget that trims the fat. At some point you may also have to create a crisis budget—if a member of your family loses his or her job, for example. You can use the budget worksheet on the following pages to get started.

---

## BUDGET WORKSHEET

### MONTHLY INCOME   (A)

Salary

Investment income

Child support

Alimony

Free-lance

Other

MONTHLY TOTAL   (A)_____

## BUDGET WORKSHEET

## FIXED EXPENSES  (B)

Housing (mortgage/rent)

Taxes (FICA, federal, state)

Automobile loans

Misc. Loans/leases

Insurance premiums

    Home
    Life
    Automobile
    Disability

Child support payments

Alimony

Other

MONTHLY TOTAL  (B)_____

## VARIABLE EXPENSES  (C)

Groceries

Medical and dental

Child care and baby-sitting

Commutation:
    Ticket
    Parking, tolls
    Bus fare
    Garage

Utilities:
    Oil
    Gas
    Electric
    Water

Telephone

Sewer/garbage pickup

## VARIABLE EXPENSES  (C) cont.

Laundry and dry cleaning

Automobile
    Repairs
    Gasoline

House/yard upkeep

Household purchases

Clothing

Tuition

Vacation

Entertainment

Charitable donations

Other

MONTHLY TOTAL  (C)_____

## BUDGET WORKSHEET

**TOTALS**

TOTAL MONTHLY INCOME (A)          $

MONTHLY SPENDING (B + C)          $

Difference: (A) − (B + C)          $

The difference is the dollar amount you can save each month. If it is a negative number, then you *must* cut back some of your variable expenses. Aim to save 5–10% of your take-home pay, but saving 1% is better than zero.

## SIX STEPS TO TAKE RIGHT NOW

Now that you know what a recession is and where to get accurate information about it, make the most of what you've learned. Ease the impact of tough times ahead by following these six steps:

Step 1. Discuss the recession with the members of your family. If all of you understand what's happening to the economy, then budgeting, cutting back, and looking for work will be easier and more effective.

Step 2. Be realistic. Recessions eventually have an impact on nearly everyone.

Step 3. Stop outrageous spending.

Step 4. Begin building up cash reserves.

Step 5. Safeguard your job: Be on time; be enthusiastic; work a little harder; stay a little later; upgrade your skills or get more education; accept lateral move offers; don't be unrealistically demanding.

Step 6. Read the rest of this book.

# 2

# Where to Put Your Money and When

In boom times, when the economy is expanding, it's easy to figure out where to invest your money because nearly everything goes up in value, and even if certain stocks or mutual funds tumble, eventually they will bounce back—provided they were sound investments. In a recession the situation changes dramatically and determining where to put your money is much more difficult, although not impossible.

Regardless of the depth and direction of the recession, everyone should build savings and reduce debt to weather the storm. Traditionally, it is considered optimal to have three months of living expenses in savings. During recessionary times, you might want to double this amount. Another savings strategy is to save 5–10% of your pretax income each year. (If you didn't read the section on savings in Chapter 1, page 17, you should go back and read it now.) <u>Your emergency savings should be placed where you can reach it quickly—and where it is extremely safe.</u>

Treasury bills, bank certificates of deposit, and high-yielding money market mutual funds are the best parking places for cash one might need within six months to a year. As Jay Goldinger, author of *Early Warning Wire*, a newsletter predicting ecomomic trends (213-858-5160), says, during tricky times, the best advice is "just try to survive. For when uncertainty ends and you can see a sound direction, you'll have the cash to make intelligent investments. Until then, play it safe with liquid investments."

Investments in stocks and bonds is still a viable option during a recession, but make certain that you can live with the risks. In this chapter, we will discuss what you should do with real estate, stocks, bonds, savings accounts, and other investments as the U.S. moves through these tough times.

## SAFE PLACES FOR YOUR CASH

Even with the recession in our backyard, trouble in the Middle East, and the possibility of more bank failures, there are safe investments for your money. Stick to those that have firm financial backing—such as U.S. Treasuries and stocks with clean balance sheets and low debt. Steer clear of anything that smacks of debt—junk bonds and highly leveraged companies—or investments you don't understand. If you're ultraconservative or if your savings are small and liquidity is important, put your money into investments that mature in a year or less. CDs, money market mutual funds, and U.S. Treasury issues are the best bet for safety.

## CERTIFICATES OF DEPOSIT

CDs are issued by most banks and commonly mature in three and six months, and at one, two, and five years. You can usually buy a CD for $500 or less. They are offered at a fixed rate of interest and rates rise with the length of maturity.Unlike a money market fund, which is extremely liquid, a CD cashed in before its maturity incurs a penalty ranging from one month's to six months' interest. Rates and terms vary widely so it pays to comparison shop. Find out if the CD offers simple or compound interest. When interest is figured daily, or compounded, the CD will yield more money; essentially this means you will earn interest on your interest earnings.

28

Since bank CDs are insured by the Federal Deposit Insurance Corporation (FDIC) for up to $100,000, they are safe choices. Nonetheless, buy CDs only from banks with high-grade safety ratings. Although the FDIC will fully reimburse you for a CD of $100,000 or less, if the bank defaulted, there could be a delay of several weeks.

$$ ACTION TIP: Bank CDs are also sold by brokers. Call several as well as your local bank to compare rates. Then check the Friday *Wall Street Journal* for listings of the nation's highest-yielding CDs.

With some 1,600 of the nation's banks and S&Ls on regulators' lists of troubled institutions, savers need to select CDs more carefully than ever. To determine how safe a bank is, for a modest fee Veribanc, Inc. will send you a financial evaluation of any bank or savings and loan. Contact Veribanc, Inc., P.O. Box 461, Wakefield, MA 01880, 800-442-2657 or 617-245-8370. For information on FDIC insurance, call consumer hotline: 800-424-5488.

When interest rates are low, buy six-month to one-year CDs, then as they come due reinvest them in higher-yielding CDs. When rates are at record highs, buy the longest-term CDs. During a recession, rates on three- and six-month CDs tend to fall the most since more people seek out these liquid accounts. And, stock investors use them to park cash during the bear market.

## MONEY MARKET MUTUAL FUNDS

Money market mutual funds are run by companies that pool money from thousands of investors and, under professional management, put it in "cash equivalents"—Treasury bills, commercial paper from the nation's top-rated corporations, jumbo bank CDs, and government-agency debt. Such holdings mature quickly—in thirty to ninety days; this, in combination with their high quality, makes money funds extremely safe. These funds are entirely liquid—you can cash them in at any time. Interest rates are variable and calculated daily. Most funds offer checkwriting privileges, though often with a $100 or $500 per check minimum.

Although these funds are traditionally regarded as ultrasafe, they are not FDIC-insured and a recession increases the chances that corporations could default on their commercial paper, one of the major assets of most money funds. Over the past several years, eight issuers have defaulted on $677 million of commercial paper. Thus far the funds' sponsors have absorbed the losses. For instance, T. Rowe Price bought $34 million of questionable paper from its fund when Mortgage & Realty Trust, a real estate investment trust, defaulted in April of 1990. If you are concerned about this possibility, money market funds that hold Treasury bills and short-term paper issued by government agencies are basically free from such risk. Their yields, in many cases, are further enhanced by the fact that part of their dividends are exempt from state and local taxes in most but not all states. This adds the equivalent of a half a percentage point to the funds' yields.

A few money funds consistently pay higher rates than others; see the box below.

## SAFE HARBORS
### (Taxable, high yielding funds)

| Fund | Minimum | Yield* |
|------|---------|--------|
| Fidelity Spartan (800-544-8888) | $20,000 | 7.99% |
| Dreyfus Worldwide Dollar MMF (800-645-6561) | 2,500 | 8.13 |
| Alger Portfolio (800-992-3863) | 1,000 | 8.09 |
| Flex Fund (800-325-FLEX) | 2,500 | 8.00 |
| Twentieth Century Cash Reserve (800-345-2021) | none | 7.17 |

*Yields as of January 14, 1991. (7 day compound effective)

$$ ACTION TIP: *Donoghue's Money Letter* covers money market funds as well as mutual fund families. Contact P.O. Box 8008, Holliston, MA 01746; 800-343-5413. Cost of one-year subscription is $99. IBC Donoghue's Money Fund Tables are published in over seventy newspapers across the country.


## U.S. TREASURY ISSUES

This investment requires no research, pays competitive rates, and is extremely safe—ideal qualities during a recession. There are three forms of Treasuries: T-bills, T-notes, and T-bonds. All are backed by the government and interest earned is free from state and local, although not federal, taxes. Two factors govern the choice of which Treasury issue to buy: the amount you have to invest and the length of time you can tie it up. All Treasuries can be sold before maturity, but if interest rates have gone up, the value of your issues will have dropped.

The shortest-term issues, *T-bills*, mature in thirteen, twenty-six, or fifty-two weeks. The drawback for many investors is that the minimum investment is $10,000, going up by $5,000 increments. The bills sell at a discount, meaning that in place of interest payments, investors buy at a percentage of face value and receive the full value when the bills mature.

U.S. *Treasury notes* mature in one to ten years and pay out a fixed rate of interest twice a year. The minimum investment is $1,000 for notes maturing in four years or more and $5,000 for those maturing in less than four.

U.S. *Treasury bonds* are merely a "longer" version of T-notes. They mature in ten to thirty years. Like T-notes, they are sold with a locked-in rate of interest, which is paid twice a year. The minimum investment is $1,000.

$$ ACTION TIP: Treasuries can be purchased from stockbrokers for a fee. But to save money, buy them from Federal

Reserve banks and their branches at no cost. Call 202-287-4113 or write to the Bureau of Public Debt, Correspondence Branch, Room 429, 1300 C Street, SW, Washington, DC 20239-0001.

If shorter-term Treasury minimums investments are too high, you can buy shares in a mutual fund such as Benham's Capital Preservation (minimum: $1,000; 800-472-3389) or Rushmore's Fund for Government Investors (minimum: $2,500; 800-343-3355) which are Treasury-only funds. Neuberger & Berman's Limited Maturity Bond Fund (800-877-9700) invests not only in U.S. Treasuries, but in high-grade corporate bonds.

# BANK MONEY MARKET ACCOUNTS AND PASSBOOK SAVINGS

These types of savings accounts are convenient but rates are low. Money market accounts yield 1½–2½ percentage points less than money market mutual funds, and passbook savings are little better than storing your money under your mattress—they pay anywhere from 4½ to 5½%. Of course, these are both FDIC-insured. Remember, a CD is, too.

## Savings & Loans and Credit Unions

The failure of a number of S&Ls has made everyone nervous, and with good reason. If you have money in an S&L, check immediately to see if it is covered by the SAIF, the Savings Association Insurance Fund, which guarantees depositors for up to $100,000.

If you don't have money in an S&L, don't start now. In most cases, when the unthinkable happens and an S&L fails, a solvent and healthy institution takes over the failed S&L's assets and liabilities.

For example, in April 1990, when Seamen's Bank for Savings in New York collapsed, its 13 branches—valued at about $2.1 billion—were sold to Chase Manhattan Bank and accounts were simply transferred. Depositors had access to their money the next day.

However, in some cases deposits are frozen if a buyer is not readily available. Or, if assets are liquidated, there is a delay before depositors can get their money.

$$ ACTION TIP: If in doubt about an S&L, contact Veribanc (see page 29) and the Savings Association Insurance Fund, located at 550 17th Street, Washington, DC 20429; 800-424-5488.

 Credit unions, too, have run into problems. To avoid uncertainty, use a credit union that is federally chartered and insures accounts up to $100,000 through the National Credit Union Share Insurance Fund.

## STOCKS

When a company wants to raise capital, it can borrow money from a bank, sell bonds, or issue stocks to the public. Stocks are sold to the public in two steps: first in an initial public offering (IPO), which is called the primary market, and thereafter to other investors in the secondary market, through the stock exchanges.

A stock is a security that represents fractional ownership in a corporation. In order to document the fact that people own shares, the company issues a stock certificate which shows how many shares have been purchased by that person.

If you're going to get involved in the stock market, ignore hot tips and so-called inside rumors overheard at your gym or on the tennis court. Instead bear in mind that there are only three things a stock can do: It can go up in price; it can go down in price; or it can stay the same. The only way to make money with a stock is though price appreciation and/or dividends.

The market determines capital appreciation. If people like the stock and want to buy it, the price moves up. But it is the company's board of directors that determines whether or not dividends will be paid.

Dividends, which are paid quarterly to shareholders, are generally paid out of the company's profits. Whatever is not paid out in dividends is reinvested in the company.

Dividends vary from company to company. Some never pay dividends. Those that consistently pay out high dividends, such as utility companies, are known as *income stocks*. The current dividend divided by the price of a share is called the *yield*.

Some corporations reinvest most of their profits in order to help the business expand and pay little or no dividends. These are known as *growth stocks*. Investors buy them because they expect the company to grow and the price of the stock to grow along with it.

A word about the secondary market. Once a company's first or initial public offering is sold, its shares then trade in the secondary market.

The secondary market is not any one place, but includes the New York and American stock exchanges (both located in New York City), and a handful of regional stock exchanges in large cities plus the over-the-counter market. At a stock exchange, listed stocks—those approved by the exchange for trading—are bought and sold. The exchanges do not own the stocks nor do they influences the prices; they merely function as an auction place for stocks.

Prices are determined by buyers and sellers, and a stock's price at any given time depends on the amount people are willing to pay for it. Each stock has an identifying symbol consisting of letters that stockbrokers use to punch in on their computers to get current prices. The symbol for Clorox, for example, is CLX; for International Business Machines, IBM.

## BONDS

Another way corporations raise money is by selling bonds to investors with the promise to pay back the face value of the bond plus interest at the date of maturity. The face value of most bonds is $1,000—the price you'll pay when they are first issued. Thereafter, just like stocks, bond prices rise and fall.

The corporation sets the interest rate—called the coupon rate—which is fixed and based on the cost of money at the time the bonds are issued. Bonds can be issued for almost any number of years, although twenty and thirty years are typical maximums. Those with maturities under ten years are called notes.

When reading bond quotes in the paper, you'll see that they are not quoted at $1,000, which is face value, but rather on the basis of 100. Always add another zero to the figure to get the actual cash price you must pay.

Although bonds are recommended primarily for their interest income, the bond market is also volatile. If interest rates rise and you need to sell your bonds prior to maturity, you'll face a loss; the value of the bonds will have dropped because newer bonds, paying higher coupon rates, will be more prized.

Many American corporations issue bonds on a continuous basis. They tend to pay higher yields than U.S. Treasuries because they are not backed by the government and thus are considered higher in risk. You can easily determine the quality of a bond by checking its rating in Moody's or Standard & Poor's, two independent rating services. To decrease default risk, stick to A-rated bonds. To avoid interest rate risk—the risk that rates will go up while you're locked in to issues with lower yields—purchase short to intermediate length notes.

Some corporate bonds have what is known as a "call provision," which allows the issuer to redeem the bond prior to scheduled maturity. Bonds have a call price that is usually higher than the face value in order to compensate the bond owner for the loss of future interest income. Check with your broker to see if your bond can be called.

## Investment Choices

| Investment | Risk Level | Definition |
|---|---|---|
| • Savings Account | Low | Account in which deposited funds earn interest. |
| • Money Market Deposit Accounts | Low | Account that pays market rates and allows limited third-party transactions; federally insured. |
| • Certificate of Deposit (CD) | Low | Receipt sold in exchange for a sum of money left in a bank for a set period of time. Earns interest. |
| • Money Market Mutual Funds | Low | Pooled money of many investors put into a company that buys short-term money market securities that are high in safety; not federally insured. |
| • EE Savings Bonds | Low | A non-marketable obligation of the U.S. Treasury aimed at small investors. |
| • Treasury Bills, Notes, and Bonds | Low | Securities of the U.S. Treasury with various maturities. |

| Where to Buy | Questions to Ask |
|---|---|
| ✓ Banks, Credit Unions, S&L | • What is the interest rate? |
| | • How often is it compounded? |
| | • Are you federally insured? |
| ✓ Banks, Credit Unions, S&L | • What is the interest rate? |
| | • What is it based on? |
| | • How often does it change? |
| ✓ Banks, Credit Unions, S&L, Stockbroker | • How much will I have at maturity? |
| | • Can I roll over my CD at the same rate or higher? |
| | • Is there an early-withdrawal penalty? |
| Mutual Funds, Stockbroker | • What is the yield? |
| | • How long does it take to get my money out? |
| | • Will you wire money to my bank? |
| Banks, S&L, Federal Reserve banks and branches, U.S. Bureau of Public Debt | • What is the current rate? |
| | • How long must I hold bonds to get that rate? |
| | • When do bonds mature? |
| | • Will I pay taxes on the interest? |
| Stockbrokers, Federal Reserve banks and branches | • What is the current rate? |
| | • How do I redeem early? |
| | • What is the purchase price and fee? |

| Investment | Risk Level | Definition |
|---|---|---|
| • Stocks | | Security that repre- |
|   Blue Chip | Medium | sents ownership in |
|   Growth Stocks | High | a corporation. |
| | | |
| • Bonds | | Debt obligations |
|   A Rated | Medium | generally issued by |
|   Below A Rated | Medium to High | large corporations. |
|   Junk or High Yield | High | |
| | | |
| • Mutual Funds | | Pooled money of |
|   Treasury Issues | Low | many investors to |
|   Blue Chip Stocks | Medium | buy a variety of |
|   Growth Stocks | High | securities. Some |
|   High Yield Bonds | High | funds invest in |
|   A Rated Bonds | Medium | stocks, some in |
|   Below A Rated Bonds | Medium to High | bonds, and some in both. |

| *Where to Buy* | *Questions to Ask* |
|---|---|
| Stockbroker | • What is your commission?<br>• What is the dividend?<br>• Do I keep my certificate? |
| Stockbroker | • What is your commission?<br>• Can the bond be called in early—before maturity?<br>• What is the yield? |
| Mutual Funds, Stockbroker | • What is the fund's total return?<br>• How risky is it?<br>• What are all the fees? |

## FIVE ECONOMIC SCENARIOS
## AND THEIR IMPACT ON INVESTMENTS

Once you have found safe havens and sound investments for your money, you still have to monitor the economic situation as it changes and be prepared to react if:

- Interest rates fall.
- Interest rates rise.
- War is declared.
- The economy starts to recover.
- The economy falters more.

In the remainder of this chapter, all of the above contingencies are addressed in regard to their affect on real estate, stocks, bonds, collectibles, gold, and cash and cash equivalents. An arrow heading upward ( ↑ ) indicates the current economic situation will most likely help boost the price of the investment, while an arrow pointing down ( ↓ ) indicates that the investment will probably drop in price.

## WHAT TO DO IF INTEREST RATES FALL

**Real Estate**  ↓ ↑

Falling interest rates typically make it easier to sell a house because mortgages are available at appealing rates. But during this financial recession, banks have been battered with poor real estate loans and mortgages are tough for most people to obtain. This condition may change due to some government support or after painful bank failures and consolidations.

$$ ACTION TIP: If you're trying to sell but don't have to do so immediately, wait out the recession until values rise. In the meantime, if you can afford to buy, this is the time to do it. The slump in residential and commercial property in many

parts of the country has led to a large number of distressed sales. The residential auction, once a rarity, is gaining in popularity as a large inventory of foreclosure properties come to market. Public notices of default sales are posted at city halls and announced in local newspapers. Thanks to the S&L debacle, the federal government is now one of the country's biggest real estate brokers and is auctioning thousands of homes through the Resolution Trust Corporation (RTC). For a list of repossessed properties in your area, call 800-782-3006 or 800-431-0600. There is a $5 fee for the information. Government agencies and mortgage lenders also often list with local brokers; many pay closing costs or accept smaller than usual down payments. For a list of foreclosed properties offered by Fannie Mae (Federal National Mortgage Association), call 800-553-4636.

In addition, blocks of newly constructed homes also go up for auction when builders can't sell them. Look for "absolute auctions," where the property will be sold no matter how low the lowest bid. Always visit the property first and be prepared financially. Know the size of the mortgage you can obtain before bidding.

*Buying in an unknown area.* Whether it's rental property or a home for yourself, get a "destination appraisal" before buying blind in an unknown market. Otherwise you could move in and find out later that a shopping mall is going in nearby. These pre-purchase appraisals ($200 to $400) let buyers know about hidden problems as well as give them a gauge regarding fair prices. To find a qualified appraiser, call the Society of Real Estate Appraisers, 800-331-7732 and request "Directory of Designated Members."

*Help for First-Time Buyers.* If you're hesitating to buy because the downpayment would leave you strapped to renovate, lenders in a number of major cities are now combining first mortgages with home repair loans in a single 5% downpayment package. The G.E. Community Home Improvement Loan is sponsored by the Federal National Mortgage

Association (800-876-4343). To qualify, your family must have an income that is no more than 15% above the local median.

*If you're a trade-up buyer*. Price your old home to sell, setting the price at a realistic level. Then, as you house-hunt, study the prices in the area. To judge if prices are still heading down, find out how long it's taking to unload them. If the average time is lengthening, the real estate market has not hit bottom.

*Finding the lowest-rate mortgage*. Contact HSH Associates (800-873-2837 or 201-838-3330), which tracks mortgage listings for most areas of the country. One survey is $18. Another source of help is seller financing. If a seller is desperate, they may give you excellent terms. Even if a house is not advertised with seller financing, it doesn't hurt to ask. *Caution*: Sellers' mortgages are often short-term and at the end the loan may balloon—meaning the entire balance is due. You should also check the default clause in the contract: Can the seller take back the property if you don't meet the payments?

## Stocks ↑

Lower interest rates are a plus for stocks; they make it less expensive for businesses to borrow money, which they do in order to expand. In turn, business conditions become healthier, corporate profits rise, the prices of stocks rise, and dividends are often increased. When rates are high, say 9% or more, bonds, CDs, U.S. Treasury securities, and money market accounts are more attractive than stocks and these interest-bearing accounts pull people out of the stock market. Then when rates fall, growth stocks are more appealing than interest-paying investments because they offer both appreciation and, in many cases, solid dividends.

By their very nature, stocks are long-term investments

which rise in price over time as company earnings and dividends grow. An investor in common stock simply cannot buy on January 1st and sell on December 31st and automatically expect to have a profit. The greatest benefits of owning solid stocks, such as PepsiCo or Procter & Gamble (see page 63), come from being a long-term stockholder. For example, four years ago PepsiCo was selling at $10 per share; today, even in the recession, its shares are $26. Likewise, Procter & Gamble has moved from $48 per share to $86 over a three-year period. Although a recession can hurt individual stocks, the best ones retain their value and bounce back. Of course, it's a good buying opportunity when prices are down.

$$ ACTION TIP: When interest rates start to fall, buy blue-chip stocks (see lists on pages 60–64) or a blue-chip mutual fund.

## Bonds ⬆

Lower interest rates are also good for bonds. *Existing* bonds, paying the old higher rates, become more valuable in terms of resale because new bonds pay lower rates. For example, you buy a bond which pays 9% ($90 per year for a $1,000 bond) for $1,000. It matures (is paid off) in ten years. After you make your purchase, rates fall to 8%. How much is your bond now worth should you choose to cash it in? The answer is around $1,070 or a $70 premium because new bonds pay only $80 per year and yours pays $90. So, when interest rates fall, bonds get a ( ⬆ ).

$$ ACTION TIP: Hold on to your old bonds and invest the interest payments. The Federal Reserve Board usually tries to make borrowing cheaper in a recession in order to stimulate economic growth. As rates start to drop, new bonds will give lower yields. Purchase two- to four-year Treasury notes. The advantage of these short maturities is that if interest rates rise, the principal from maturing notes can be reinvested at

newer, higher rates. If yields on longer-term Treasuries approach 10%, however, buy longer-term Treasuries in order to lock in high rates.

$$ ACTION TIP: Ask your broker about Refcorps, a thirty-year bond issued by the government's Resolution Funding Corp to help finance the S&L bailout. If Refcorp cannot pay interest on the bonds, the Treasury is required to make up the difference.

## Collectibles ↑

When interest rates fall, hold on to collectibles and antiques. They will continue to appreciate in value. Perhaps you meant to sell your old grandfather clock when rates were high, say at 10%. In fact, you were offered $5,000. You planned to invest the $5,000 at 10%. But now the rate has fallen to 7.5%. Hold on to the clock and let it keep ticking and appreciating.

## Gold ↓ ↑

Traditionally, gold prices move up in response to fears about inflation, economic problems, political upheavals, wars, and revolutions. In fact, gold is regarded as the traditional hedge against inflation because many people feel it is the only true store of value. Gold is thought of as insurance. But gold is a *negative* investment: Every dollar you invest in gold costs you the amount of money you could earn if that money were earning interest in a bank, Treasury bill, money market fund, or elsewhere. So when interest rates fall, the cost of holding gold is less detrimental than when rates rise. (See box on "How to Buy Gold," page 46.)

$$ ACTION TIP: Many financial advisors recommend that 3–5% of each person's portfolio should be in gold to

hedge against a world monetary crisis or double-digit inflation. Buy a small amount of bullion, gold stocks, or gold mutual funds as rates fall and tuck it away. Fear of oil-supply interruptions is one of the reasons investors keep some of their portfolio in gold.

## Cash ↓

Cash, bank deposits, certificates of deposit (CDs), money market mutual funds, and Treasury bills are known as cash or cash equivalents. When interest rates are falling, these are worth less because their yields are falling. Lower interest rates also make the dollar a less appealing currency in which to hold all one's investments. Slower growth in the U.S. economy eventually has the effect of further reducing the global purchasing power of the dollar.

$$ ACTION TIP: Buy shares in an international cash mutual fund. Like domestic money funds, these invest in safe short-term paper. When the dollar drops, their returns increase. Huntington Advisers in Pasadena, California (800-354-4111), manages three international cash portfolios. Its High-Income Currency Portfolio, which invests in money market securities of the U.S., Canada, and five countries with the highest short-term rates, consistently has a high yield. Call for current figures.

$$ ACTION TIP: In general, reposition your cash assets into stocks, bonds (or mutual funds), collectibles, or a small amount of gold when rates fall.

SUMMARY: When interest rates fall = Real estate ( ↓ ↑ )
Stocks        ( ↑ )
Bonds        ( ↑ )
Collectibles ( ↑ )
Gold          ( ↓ ↑ )
Cash          ( ↓ )

# HOW TO BUY GOLD

There are several ways to buy gold: You can purchase *gold bullion* bars from larger banks, brokerage firms, and major dealers, and, if you like, take physical possession, storing them in your safe-deposit box or burying them in your backyard. A less cumbersome and more practical arrangement is to purchase a *certificate* indicating that you own the metal and to let a dealer store it for you in a vault. Certificate minimums are usually $1,000. They are sold roughly 3% over the price of the metal; plus there's an annual storage fee of approximately 1%.

*Gold bullion coins*, such as the American Gold Eagle, Canadian Mapleleaf, Australian Nugget, Mexican 50-peso, Austrian 100-Corono, Hungarian Corona, and Chinese Panda are popular; but bear in mind they have no numismatic or collectors' value and their price is based on the value of the gold content. They should not be confused with rare coins whose value is based on their age, rarity, condition, and popularity.

*Mutual funds* offer a way to participate in gold without the hassle of holding gold bars or selecting individual mining company stock. Because of the potential production disruption, the moral issue of apartheid, and other problems in the South African mines, we suggest funds that avoid heavy commitments in that country. NOTE: Funds are not a "pure play"; that is, you are buying partial shares of stocks of companies that mine metals, not the metal itself. Profits depend on how well the fund is managed and the stock market.

*Gold stocks* of mining companies offer potential price appreciation and dividend income, yet at the same time leave you subject to stock market risks, political upheavals, and labor unrest.

$$ ACTION TIP: Although you should never succumb to a high-pressure salesman, you can indeed buy bullion bars and coins by phone from reliable dealers whom you know; however, check several for prices and fees first.

- *Citibank's Precious Metals Division* allows clients to use their Visa or MasterCard to buy gold. Call 800-223-1080. The bank's twenty-four-hour hot line gives the latest spot prices: 302-427-4700.
- *Merrill Lynch's "Blueprint"* program has a minimum purchase of only $100 with $50 thereafter. Call 800-637-3766.
- *Benham Certified Metals* has a discount division. The minimum purchase for gold is $2,000. Call 800-447-4653.
- *Rhode Island Hospital Trust National Bank* of Providence sells coins, bars, and certificates. It also has an accumulation account for $100 per month. Call 800-343-8419 or 401-278-7595.

NOTE: For a directory of recommended dealers, contact the Industry Council for Tangible Assets at 202-783-3500.

## WHAT TO DO IF INTEREST RATES RISE

### Real Estate ↓

Housing and most types of real estate become less valuable when interest rates rise, primarily because mortgages, which are essential to most buyers, cost more. If this cost rises too much, potential buyers are shut out of the market. Fewer buyers, of course, means lower prices.

### Stocks ↓

Higher interest rates hurt stock prices because long-term stockholders get restless as they see bonds, CDs, and money market funds paying increasingly higher yields than the dividends on their stock. Many investors sell their stocks and move their money into interest-bearing investments. If selling is widespread, stocks fall even further in price. So as a rule, when rates rise, returns on common stocks do not yield as much as newly issued bonds.

## Bonds ↓

Higher interest rates are also a negative for *existing* bonds. Investors purchase new bonds which offer higher rates and the older bonds' resale value falls to a discount (below $1,000) in order to adjust to the new higher rates.

$$ ACTION TIP: Don't sell your existing bonds and bond mutual funds. Instead, add to them to lock in the new, higher yields.

## Collectibles ↓

Collectibles and antiques suffer in value when interest rates rise. As much as you love your grandfather clock, you can consider selling it now and putting the proceeds into a higher-yielding investment.

NOTE: At times in the past when the Federal Reserve Bank pushed interest rates up in order to stem the forces of inflation, the inflationary fever was so great that antiques and collectibles rose in price. But this price rise was largely due to inflationary fears.

## Gold ↓

Gold prices fall during periods of rising interest rates. As we explained above, gold is a *negative* investment. It costs money to own because you could be earning interest on your money if it were invested elsewhere, say in bonds. This is particularly true when rates rise.

NOTE: Of course, if higher interest rates are due to a war, revolution, or major economic disruption, then the price of gold will rise in the short run as people seek an alternative to paper currency.

**$$ ACTION TIP:** If you own gold, keep it but don't add to it as interest rates rise.

**Cash**

Cash, short-term CDs, three- and six-month Treasury bills, and money market mutual funds are just great when interest rates rise. Now you can take these liquid funds and invest them in any of the above categories at lower and more favorable prices. Bonds yield higher interest returns, stocks are lower in price, and gold, antiques, and real estate are also on the bargain counter.

SUMMARY: When interest rates rise = Real estate ( ↓ )
Stocks ( ↓ )
Bonds ( ↓ )
Collectibles ( ↓ )
Gold ( ↓ )
Cash ( ↑ )


## WHAT TO DO IF WAR IS DECLARED

As we move into the decade of the 1990s, there are three principal industrial areas of the world: (1) the Pacific Basin, which includes Japan and the newly industrialized countries (NICs) of Korea, Taiwan, and Hong Kong; (2) Western Europe; and (3) the United States. Any war or major disruption which severely impacts one or more of these three areas is real war in economic terms. Suffering and tragedy of course occur in other wars, but the economic impact is far less.

The current Persian Gulf conflict involves the interests of all three areas, whether those interests are strictly economic, such as Japan's, or economic and military, such as the United

States' and Great Britain's. If the conflict continues and a significant number of oil facilities are crippled oil prices will skyrocket.

One other possible concern is Soviet Russia. If internal revolutions continue to spread, the Soviet Union could collapse from within. The end result would be chaos. A wave of refugees would pour through Eastern Europe into the Western European countries, choking refugee facilities and causing widespread economic panic.

These three situations would cause severe economic changes, as opposed to a minor military operation, such as took place under President Reagan in Grenada. But what happens to you and your financial life if war breaks out?

## Real Estate  ↑ ↓

If the war causes immediate shortages of gasoline and home heating oil, then the first reaction is a negative one for those in suburban, country, and beach houses, and especially for rural Americans who are totally dependent on gasoline. On the other hand, wars are good for a number of businesses, so more people will have jobs, and consequently be making money.

$$ ACTION TIP: It's a bit of a standoff for real estate, so we give both an up and a down arrow. If you're seeking to buy, this is a good time; if you're trying to sell you may want to wait for higher prices.

## Stocks  ↑ ↓

War is always good for some stocks. They may not be the stocks you own because wars create a new ball game with new winners (oil producers, aerospace companies, war-related chemical companies) and some new losers (for example, refinery builders who are building big refineries in Saudi Arabia, an airline which has just started a new route to Soviet Russia, companies building new factories in "East" Germany). So during a war stocks gets a mixed bag of two arrows ( ↓ .↑ ).

$$ ACTION TIP: If you don't mind a moderate amount of risk, buy a few shares of aerospace and energy stocks or a mutual fund specializing in energy stocks, technically known as a "sector" fund. The no-fee mutual fund groups with energy sector funds are: Fidelity (800-544-8888), Financial Strategic (800-525-8085), T. Rowe Price (800-638-5660), and Vanguard (800-662-7447). Among the stocks to consider are General Dynamics, Lockheed, and Petroleum & Resources Fund, a closed-end fund trading on the New York Stock Exchange. Additional energy stocks and bonds are discussed in Chapters 3 and 6.

## Bonds ↓

Bonds get a straight arrow down. War is *not* good for bonds. Wars are inflationary, sometimes causing shortages, and everyone shows a strong preference for cash and cash equivalents.

$$ ACTION TIP: It we have a war, sell your bonds and stay in cash, or put some of your assets in the two sector fund areas listed above.

## Collectibles ↑

Collectibles and antiques do not immediately run up in price at the outbreak of war. But just wait a while. As previously stated, wars are usually inflationary, causing corporate profits, employment, and consumer prices to rise. Higher inflation and expanding industrial production will boost the prices of collectibles if the war lasts long enough.

**$$ ACTION TIP:** Hold on to that grandfather clock if a war starts.

## Gold ⬆

When there is panic in the streets, people like to have gold in their safe deposit vaults. The more disruption, inflation, and uncertainty about the future there is, the more investors turn to gold. The price of gold usually moves upward at the first onset of a new and frightening disruption. If the situation is really bad and it appears as if it will get worse, then hang on to gold. But if political discord settles down into a stalemate or if negotiations for peace begin, then the price for gold will start to fall. On the other hand, if the war looks like it will bring on a severe spending and inflationary era (for example, another Vietnam) then keep some of your gold as an inflation hedge.

## Cash ⬆

Cash and cash equivalents are the number-one preference during a war or even during a serious threat of war. "Get me out," investors tell their stockbrokers, "and into cash." Headlines scream: STOCKS PLUMMET AS WAR ERUPTS.

**$$ ACTION TIP:** If you feel war is around the corner, get as liquid as possible and reduce stock and bond holdings. Later on you may reposition your cash into oil or aerospace stocks or the safer U.S. Treasury short-term notes. But at first blush, cash is best.

SUMMARY: If war is declared =

| | |
|---|---|
| Real estate | ( ⬇ ⬆ ) |
| Stocks | ( ⬇ ) |
| Bonds | ( ⬇ ) |
| Collectibles | ( ⬆ ) |
| Gold | ( ⬆ ) |
| Cash | ( ⬆ ) |

## WHAT TO DO IF THE ECONOMY
## STARTS TO RECOVER

### Real Estate | ↑ |

When the economy starts to recover, prices of real estate head back up as well. More employment, easier credit, and increased industrial production boost the number of people who can afford to buy houses and (except for our 1990–1991 atypical situation) the number of banks wanting to lend them mortgage money.

$$ ACTION TIP: If you've been thinking of selling your home, hold on a bit longer and monitor the real estate market. It should continue to improve; sell when you believe the prices in your area have recovered from the recession.

### Stocks | ↑ |

Stock prices improve when the economy starts to expand. Employment rises, consumer sentiment improves, and soon consumer spending increases, thus starting the ball rolling for industrial expansion and a rise in corporate profits. All of these factors eventually lead to higher earnings for major corporations and higher stock prices. Stocks get a definite arrow up ( ↑ ). Switch your money market funds to a blue-chip stock fund when the economy starts to recover.

### Bonds | ↓ |

Bonds do not do as well during expansions as they do during recessions. There are two reasons for this: One, new bonds will be paying higher interest rates as the expanding economy creates competition among corporate borrowers for new money with which to fuel their expansions. This lowers the value of your existing bonds which are locked into lower rates. And two, stocks, which rise as the economy recovers, will offer a more attractive investment alternative.

$$ ACTION TIP: If you are a conservative investor and want only to invest in bonds, then let the expansion move along a little and look for higher rates of interest as the expansion continues.

## Collectibles ↑

Collectibles find a better market when the economy recovers. There are more people working, more corporate executives commanding top salaries, and more business people smiling over their expanding profits. When the expansion heats up, there will be more potential buyers who can't live without your clock. You should try to sell when the expansion reaches its peak.

## Gold ↓

Unless the new recovery in the economy is also highly inflationary, you won't want to buy or hold gold during this period. Gold is best reserved for counterbalancing fears of inflation or other major disruptions. When the economy starts to recover it means that the consumer price index has fallen, worker productivity is high, and the economy looks good.

$$ ACTION TIP: Sell some of your gold or gold funds and buy quality blue-chip stocks or a blue-chip mutual fund. CAUTION: Before getting out of all your gold, heed the words of Richard Russell, noted publisher of *Dow Theory Letters* (Box 1759, La Jolla, CA 92038) 619-454-0481, who explains that the U.S. government is spending over one billion dollars every day and our public debt keeps mounting: "So the dollar isn't a store of value anymore. It is basically just a medium of transaction." Russell recommends keeping *some* of your assets in gold at all times—3–7%.

**Cash** ↓

Lastly, cash and cash equivalents are *not* the place to be when the economy starts to recover. If it is a real and noninflationary recovery, then stocks, bonds, homes, and collectibles will outperform cash.

SUMMARY: As the economy recovers = Real estate ( ↑ )
Stocks ( ↑ )
Bonds ( ↓ )
Collectibles ( ↑ )
Gold ( ↓ )
Cash ( ↓ )

## WHAT TO DO IF THE ECONOMY FALTERS MORE

As of January 1991, not all economists were agreed about the severity of this recession. The gross national product had not yet declined for two consecutive quarters, which is the classic definition of a recession, and there was some hope that we might have a "soft landing" with the economy leveling off in a way that would be painless. It might then start its recovery.

But what if these optimists are wrong and we are embarked on a recession that is broad and deep? The economy could keep on falling to a level where major banks and insurance companies become so battered by bad real estate and junk bond loans that they must choose between insolvency or forced mergers. Let's see what our financial decisions should be if things go from bad to worse:

**Real Estate** ↓

Housing prices have been hit hard in a number of parts of the U.S., with mortgages often difficult if not impossible to get. Builders and developers as well as many home owners are forced to sell at significant losses. Try to live in your house and wait until the drop in prices ends. Chances are you have no other choice. Of course, if you get a reasonable offer for your house and you want to sell, take it.

## Stocks ↓

Stocks are definitely hazardous to your financial health if the economy keeps contracting. The exception is utility stocks and very defensive (or recession-proof) industries, like health care and food, which will survive the hard times. (See Chapter 3, "Spotting Industries That Will Survive".) Yet, for the most part, stocks do not do well in a sharply contracting economy.

$$ ACTION TIP: Hold on to quality growth stocks (see Chapter 3) in good times and bad. They will perform less well during a severely declining economy, but they are still a good long-term investment.

## Bonds ↑

Bonds are a good investment if things go from bad to worse. As the economy sinks, interest rates drop and new bonds are sold with lower and lower interest rates, increasing the value of older, higher-rate bonds. So bonds get a definite arrow up ( ↑ ) during this worsening economy.

$$ ACTION TIP: Replace all but the most conservative stocks and stock funds with bond funds of the highest quality. (See pages 70–72 for suggested bonds.) Buy bonds even at what appear to be lower rates because if the economy continues to drop, interest rates will fall further.

## Collectibles ↓

Collectibles are no bargain if the economy keeps dropping

and the recession deepens. You may wish you had sold your grandfather clock while you had the chance.

## Gold  ↓ ↑

Gold is an interesting contradiction. While most people hold gold or gold funds as a hedge against inflation, there is no inflation during this scenario. On the contrary, a deepening recession is *deflationary*. Your money buys more and cash is more valuable. Why then hold gold? Because in a chaotic, declining recession, or even in a mild depression, the stronger countries of the world like Japan or the nations of Western Europe may turn to a new form of hard money based on gold. If things get as bad as all this, have mostly cash but some gold as well to hedge against an unforeseen disaster.

## Cash ↑

Cash is king in this scenario. It will buy more housing, more stocks, more bonds, and more collectibles when the bottom is finally reached. Hoard your cash during a worsening economy. Hedged with some gold, it can only become more valuable.

SUMMARY: If the economy
keeps dropping =

| | |
|---|---|
| Real estate | ( ↓ ) |
| Stocks | ( ↓ ) |
| Bonds | ( ↑ ) |
| Collectibles | ( ↓ ) |
| Gold | ( ↓ ↑ ) |
| Cash | ( ↑ ) |

# 3

# Spotting Industries
# That Will Thrive

In every phase of the business cycle—even during a recession—there are winners and there are losers. As business cycles expand, real estate developers make a fortune, auction houses sell to new tiers of wealthy customers and post record profits, and consumers buy new cars, yachts, and gems. Then suddenly there's a recession. Heavily leveraged real estate moguls declare bankruptcy, tycoons sell their jewelry, and former hotshots drive taxicabs. (According to *Money* magazine, a year ago, Donald Trump's net worth was $1.7 billion; today, it's zero.) Yet even in the midst of all this, some businesses continue to do well, even thrive, because they sell goods and services we all must have. These are the so-called "recession-resistant" industries.

Knowing something about recession-resistant industries is important for two reasons: As you'll see on the following pages, they are a wise choice for stock investments, but they are also ideal places in which to seek work. Many are located in geographically prosperous areas (see page 105 for cities that should thrive in the 1990s). If you're unemployed, look for work with companies in the general industries listed below. First check the specific companies described in this chapter—their phone numbers and addresses are listed so you can contact them directly. Next, investigate other companies in these particular business sectors. The major ones are listed, by industry, in the *Value Line Investment Survey*, available at your library. (*Value Line* gives corporate addresses and telephone numbers.)

## WHAT ARE RECESSION-RESISTANT INDUSTRIES?

Think of the things that people cannot or will not do without and you've answered the question. Listed below are the top eight categories, along with selected stocks to own within each industry during recessionary times. For additional stocks, check the company evaluations in the two leading research publications: Standard & Poor's *The Outlook* and the *Value Line Investment Survey*, available at your library and most brokerage firms.

## RECESSION-RESISTANT INDUSTRIES

- *Beverages*. Alcoholic and nonalcoholic, includes soft drinks. Sales remain strong during economic downturns.
- *Drugs*. People continue to buy medicines and over-the-counter drugs. See also: Health Care.
- *Food*. This mammoth and interconnected industry includes food production, processing and distribution, and supermarkets.
- *Health Care and Medical Supplies*. Industries that produce drugs, pharmaceuticals, and hospital supplies are increasingly essential to our aging population.
- *Household Products*. Soap, toothpaste, and personal-care products are necessities, along with household cleaning products for washing clothes, dishes, and floors.

- *Telephone and Telecommunications*. Only certain players in this industry, such as the Regional Bell Operating Companies, are truly recession-proof. (See page 65.)
- *Utilities: Gas and Electric*. In all phases of the business cycle, there's a steady, reliable demand for electricity and gas. After all, no one is willing to sit in the dark or be cold. Not all utilities are equally recession-proof, however. Those with a large component of industrial users may suffer as businesses cut back.
- *Waste Disposal*. Garbage collectors and certain companies whose activities are mandated by the government, such as hazardous waste disposal, offer services needed at all times.

## TWELVE BLUE-CHIP STOCKS (IN ALPHABETICAL ORDER)

- Abbott Laboratories   (NYSE: ABT)   Price: 42*
  Yield: 2.0%*

Abbott Labs makes drugs, diagnostic tests, intravenous solutions, and medical instruments. Drug and nutritional products are slightly more than half of its business, and the balance consists of products for hospitals and laboratories. *Annual revenues: $6 billion*. Abbott has been one of the outstanding companies in the U.S. in growth of sales and earnings, benefitting from the graying of America. Foreign business is about 34%. With long-term debt only 5% of capital, the company can withstand the economic downturn.
*Contact*: One Abbott Park Road, Abbott Park, IL 60064. Tel: 708-937-6100.

---

*All prices and yields as of January 7, 1991.

- Albertson's  (NYSE: ABS)  Price: $35*  Yield: 1.4%*

Albertson's is the sixth-largest retail grocery chain in the United States, with 523 stores in the West and South. It also operates 139 drugstores in combination with its supermarkets. *Annual revenues: $8.2 billion*. The grocery chain business is intensely competitive, but Albertson's has been one of the most successful operators in this field. By selecting its geographic areas carefully, continuously opening new stores, and going after volume discounts, it has compiled a profitable record. Long-term debt is only 14% of total capital.
*Contact*: 250 East Park Center Boulevard, Boise, ID 83706. Tel: 208-385-6200.

- Bristol-Myers Squibb  (NYSE: BMY)  Price: $64*
  Yield: 3.7%*

Bristol-Myers Squibb manufactures pharmaceuticals, proprietary medical products, and household items. Among its most popular items are Ban, Bufferin, Clairol, Drano, Enfamil, Excedrin, Nuprin, and Windex. *Annual revenues: $10 billion*. Growth prospects are excellent because of a large number of new drugs awaiting approval for marketing. Long-term debt is only 4% of total capital.
*Contact*: 345 Park Avenue, New York, NY 10154. Tel: 212-546-4000.

- Coca-Cola  (NYSE: KO)  Price: $44*  Yield: 1.8%*

Coca-Cola is the world's largest soft drink company. The food division produces over 100 products. *Annual revenues: $10.3 billion*. Because approximately 55% of sales and three-quarters of earnings come from overseas, KO stock is a strong beneficiary of weakness of the U.S. dollar against other currencies. Long-term debt is only 13% of total capital.
*Contact*: One Coca-Cola Plaza, Atlanta, GA 30313. Tel: 404-676-2121.

- Colgate-Palmolive  (NYSE: CL)  Price: $70*
  Yield: 2.6%*

Colgate is the second largest manufacturer of soaps, detergents, and toiletries in the U.S. *Annual revenues: $5.6 billion*. Its major products are Ajax, Palmolive cleansers, Ultra Brite and Colgate toothpastes, Irish Spring soap, and Hill's pet food. Foreign operations represent 64% of Colgate's total sales which impacts favorably on earnings during periods when the U.S. dollar is weak.
*Contact*: 300 Park Avenue, New York, NY 10022. Tel: 212-310-2000.


- Heinz (H. J.)  (NYSE: HNZ)  Price: $33*
  Yield: 2.9%*

H. J. Heinz manufactures soups, baked beans, baby foods, ketchup, pickles, and vinegar. Other products include Star-Kist tuna, 9-Lives cat food, OreIda frozen potatoes, and a variety of mustards and other condiments. Heinz also operates Weight-Watcher programs and sells its products. *Annual revenues: $6.5 billion*. Heinz has paid shareholders a dividend since 1911.
*Contact*: P.O. Box 57, Pittsburgh, PA 15230. Tel: 412-456-6014.


- Kellogg  (NYSE: K)  Price: $74*  Yield: 2.6%*

Kellogg, the world's largest manufacturer of ready-to-eat cereals, commands 38% of the U.S. market for cereals; within foreign markets, its market share is over 50%. *Annual revenues: $5 billion*. Its major product names are Kellogg's, Rice Krispies, Special K, Froot Loops, All-Bran, and Pop-Tarts. Foreign sales are approximately 37% of total operations and account for 31% of net income. The company has paid a dividend each year since 1923.
*Contact*: Battle Creek, MI 49016. Tel: 616-961-2765.

- PepsiCo   (NYSE: PEP)   Price: $25*   Yield: 1.6%*

PepsiCo is the second-largest soft drink producer in the world. Its major brand names are Pepsi-Cola, diet Pepsi, and Mountain Dew—produced by over 1,000 bottlers worldwide. The Frito-Lay division manufactures snacks, including Doritos and Ruffles. PEP also owns Pizza Hut, Kentucky Fried Chicken, and Taco Bell. *Annual revenues: $17.5 billion*. PepsiCo's growth is especially strong in foreign markets and its leadership position overseas is expected to continue throughout the 1990s.
*Contact*: PepsiCo World Headquarters, Purchase, NY 10577. Tel: 914-253-2000.

- Procter & Gamble   (NYSE: PG)   Price: $85*
  Yield: 2.4%*

PG is the leading soap and detergent manufacturer in the U.S. *Annual revenues: $24 billion*. The company's best-known products are Tide, Cheer, Oxydol, Crest toothpaste, Comet, Head & Shoulders shampoo, Bounty and Charmin paper products, Folger's coffee, and Noxzema shaving cream and skin lotions. In addition to its commanding position as a leading manufacturer and marketer of household products, PG derives approximately 40% of its sales from foreign markets. This enhances reported profits during years when the U.S. dollar falls in value against most foreign currencies.
*Contact*: 391 East Sixth Street, Cincinnati, OH 45202. Tel: 513-983-1100.

- Ralston Purina   (NYSE: RAL)   Price: $96*
  Yield: 1.9%*

Ralston Purina, the world's largest producer of dry dog and cat foods, also owns Continental Baking, Eveready (batteries), and Beechnut Baby Foods. Its major product names are Purina Dog and Cat Chow, Ry-Krisp, Wonder and Hostess baked products, and Energizer batteries. *Annual revenues: $7 billion*. Foreign operations are 28% of sales and contribute approximately 18% to total profits.

*Contact*: Checkerboard Square, St. Louis, MO 63164. Tel: 314-982-1000.

• Sysco   (NYSE: SYY)   Price: $33*   Yield: .8%*

Sysco distributes food and food-related products to "away-from-home" food companies, primarily restaurants, hotels, schools, factories, and nursing homes in metropolitan areas throughout the U.S. *Annual revenues: $7.5 billion*. The food service distribution business is highly fragmented and this fast-growing company continues to gain market share. Yet its current share is only about 8% (up from 2% ten years ago) so there is an abundant opportunity for Sysco to keep growing.

*Contact*: 1390 Enclave Parkway, Houston, TX 77077. Tel: 713-584-1390.

• Waste Management   (NYSE: WMX)   Price: $35*
    Yield: 1.0%*

Waste Management operates in the solid waste disposal business in over 600 communities, serving 8.3 million residential, commercial, and industrial customers. It also disposes of nuclear, chemical, and medical waste. *Annual revenues: exceed $6.2 billion*. Strong future growth should be achieved from acquisitions of smaller operators in the business and from price increases.

*Contact*: Butterfield Road, Oak Brook, IL 60521. Tel: 708-572-8800.

# THE "BABY BELL" COMPANIES

Shares of these regional telephone companies trade on the New York Stock Exchange. Yields as of January 1991 ranged from 4.5% to 6.6%. Phone company stocks traditionally hold up well during recessions and can be part of any conservative investor's portfolio.

| Company | Price* | Yield* |
|---|---|---|
| Ameritech | $65 | 5.2% |
| Bell Atlantic | 52 | 4.5 |
| Bell South | 54 | 5.0 |
| NYNEX | 70 | 6.6 |
| Pacific Telesis | 44 | 4.6 |
| Southwest Bell | 55 | 5.0 |
| U.S. West | 37 | 5.4 |

*Price and yields on January 7, 1991.

## TWENTY-TWO STEADY DIVIDEND PAYERS

One way to invest during hard times is to buy stocks of companies that have a long history of paying regular dividends. In a poor market, these stocks tend to decline less in price than those that are not dividend-oriented. This is because investors prize them and hang on to them sometimes buying additional shares when the price is down from their previous highs. The companies listed below have increased their dividends for fifteen consecutive years and debt is less than 25% of total capital. However, before purchasing these or any other stocks, read the current report in the *Value Line Investment Survey* and/or check with a reliable stockbroker or financial planner.

| Company | Lines of Business |
|---|---|
| American Business Products | Business supplies |
| American Filtrona | Tobacco filters |
| American National Insurance | Insurance |
| Aon Corp. | Insurance |
| H&R Block | Tax preparation |
| Deluxe | Check printing |
| Diebold | ATM machines |
| Duplex Products | Business forms |
| Emerson Electric | Electric parts |
| Gorman-Rupp | Pumps |
| John H. Harland Co. | Check printing |
| Hartford Steam Boiler & Insurance | Insurance |
| Hubbell Inc. | Electric parts |
| Jefferson-Pilot | Insurance |
| Lance | Snack foods |
| Minnesota Mining & Manufacturing | Tapes |
| National Gas & Oil | Natural gas supplies |
| National Service Industries | Lighting equipment |
| Pfizer | Drugs |
| Thomas & Betts | Electrical parts |
| Universal Corp. | Tobacco, insurance |
| UST Inc. | Tobacco |

# COMPANIES WITH LITTLE DEBT

These companies with strong balance sheets and little or no debt are able to confront the recession.

| Company | Line of Business |
| --- | --- |
| Abbott Laboratories | Health care products |
| Michael Baker Corp. | Engineering consultant |
| Calgon Carbon Corp. | Activated carbons |
| Dun & Bradstreet | Business publisher |
| A. G. Edwards | Securities broker |
| Federal Signal Corp. | Manufacturing of signals/signs |
| Gibson Greetings, Inc. | Greeting card manufacturer |
| Int'l Flavors & Fragrances | Perfumes and cosmetics |
| Lawson Products, Inc. | Distributes fasteners |
| Long's Drug Stores | Drugstore chain |
| Merck & Co. | Ethical drugs |
| Rollins Inc. | Pest control, fire security |
| Sanford Corp. | Office supplies |
| A. Schulman, Inc. | Plastics/resins |
| Tech/Ops Landauer, Inc. | Radiation monitoring |
| Tootsie Roll Industries | Candy |
| Weis Markets | Supermarkets |
| Wm. Wrigley, Jr. | Chewing gum |

## HIGH-YIELDING UTILITY STOCKS

These companies, appealing because of their high dividends, should continue to thrive throughout the recession.

| Company | Yield* |
| --- | --- |
| Allegheny Power | 8.6% |
| Atlanta Gas Light | 6.7 |
| Brooklyn Union Gas | 6.5 |
| FPL Group | 8.0 |
| Hawaiian Electric Company | 7.2 |
| Idaho Power Company | 7.2 |
| Ipalco Enterprises | 6.7 |
| Kansas Power & Light | 8.8 |
| National Fuel Gas | 6.1 |
| Northeast Utilities | 8.6 |
| Ohio Edison | 8.8 |
| Oklahoma Gas & Electric | 6.6 |
| Orange & Rockland | 7.5 |
| Pacificorp | 6.6 |
| Potomac Electric Power | 7.4 |
| Public Service Enterprise Group | 8.2 |
| South Jersey Industries | 7.8 |
| Southwestern Public Service | 7.8 |

*Yield on January 7, 1991.

## ENERGY AND UTILITY BONDS TO WEATHER THE STORM

During a recession, bonds are a safer bet for steady income than stocks. (Bonds pay interest twice a year and when they mature, bondholders get back the principal or face value, usually $1,000 per bond.) They have another advantage over stocks: If a corporation's earnings drop, it may reduce or even cancel the dividend on the common stock, but it is obliged to pay interest to the bondholders as well as the principal when the bonds mature, or face bankruptcy. You may wonder about the difference between bonds issued by corporations and those issued by the U.S. Treasury. Corporate bonds have higher yields than Treasury bonds, but the interest you earn is subject to federal, state, and local income taxes while interest earned on Treasuries is exempt from state and local tax in all states.

The bonds described in the following pages are all top-quality, and trade on the New York Stock Exchange. They're each rated A or better by Standard & Poor, the independent rating service based in New York. (The highest S&P rating is AAA followed by AA.) Their current yields are well above those of most CDs, money market funds, and Treasuries. If you sell your bonds before the maturity date you may get more than the face value ($1,000) if interest rates have dropped, but if interest rates have gone up you will receive less. (See page 34 for a fuller explanation of how bond prices fluctuate.) Note that current yields are given: Many corporations have a number of bonds outstanding which is why a range of yields is given rather than just one yield for each corporation.

$$ ACTION TIP: Bonds that trade on the New York Stock Exchange are listed separately from stocks in the financial pages of the newspaper. If you check for a bond's price and yield, don't be surprised if it's not there. Unlike stocks, bonds do not trade every day. *Barron's*, a financial newspaper which is published every weekend, has a record of all bonds that traded during the previous week. The fact that a bond has not traded means that the owners of bonds are happy to hold on to them and receive the income. The prices of stocks, on the other hand, are more volatile than bonds and attract traders and investors who buy and sell for as little as a point or two of profit.

# OIL COMPANY BONDS

Well-run oil companies are involved in a stable business, one that survives and often thrives in a recession because they provide products that are basic to our way of life: heating oil, jet fuel, gasoline, and other petroleum products.

• Amoco   S&P rating: AAA   Current yields: 8.6% to 9%*

Amoco is a fully integrated oil company, producing crude oil from its own wells and then refining and marketing gasoline and other petroleum products. With its acquisition of Dome Petroleum of Canada, it has a large stake in the potentially oil-rich Beaufort Sea in the Arctic Circle. *Annual revenues: $28.5 billion.*

• Atlantic Richfield   S&P rating: A+
Current yields: 8.5% to 9.5%

Atlantic Richfield, a major U.S. integrated oil company, is a key player in the production of oil from Alaska's North Slope. *Annual revenues: $16.5 billion.*

• Mobil   S&P rating: AA   Current yields: 7.2% to 8.7%

A large integrated international oil company, Mobil explores for oil throughout the world and refines and markets its products in the U.S. and most other industrialized nations. *Annual revenues: $50+ billion.*

• Chevron   S&P rating: AA   Current yields: 8.5% to 9.5%

Chevron acquired Gulf Oil Co. in 1984. Exploration activities are carried on throughout the world, and substantial stakes are held in production from Nigeria, Angola, and Indonesia. *Annual revenues: $35 billion.*

---

* Yields reported on January 7, 1991.

• Texaco    S&P rating: A+    Current yields: 8.6% to 9.1%

Texaco is a leading international integrated oil company. The present value of its oil reserves is $20 billion. *Annual revenues: $36+ billion.*

## UTILITY COMPANY BONDS

The products and services of utility companies—electricity, gas, water, and telephone—are as basic to our needs as oil. Lighting and heating our homes are absolutes, and, while there are some people who prefer to live without a telephone, there aren't very many of them!

• Bell Telephone of Pennsylvania    S&P rating: AA
  Current yields: 8.8% to 9.4%

Bell Tel of Pennsylvania is a part of the Bell Atlantic Company which in turn is one of the seven regional holding companies formed when American Telephone & Telegraph broke up in 1984. *Annual revenues for the Bell Atlantic system: $12+ billion.*

• Pacific Telephone & Telegraph    S&P rating: AA−
  Current yields: 8.6% to 9.7%

Pacific Tel. & Tel. is a subsidiary of Pacific Telesis Group, another of the seven regional holding companies that were formed with the breakup of the old American Telephone & Telegraph. The Pacific Telesis Group provides service to most of California and part of Nevada. *Annual revenues: $9.8 billion.*

• Consolidated Edison Company of New York
  S&P rating: AA    Current yields: 8.5% to 9.3%

Con Ed sells electricity and gas in New York City and Westchester County. Con Ed's financial position is regarded as one of the strongest in the electric utility industry. *Annual revenues: $5.8 billion.*

- Duke Power   S&P rating: AA —
  Current yields: 8.4% to 9.6%

Duke Power sells electricity in North and South Carolina, an area that has not been as hard-hit by the recession as the Northeast. *Annual revenues: $3.8 billion.*

- Public Service Electric & Gas Co.   S&P rating: A
  Current yields: 8% to 9.5%

Public Service Electric & Gas Co. is part of a holding company called Public Service Enterprise Group. The group sells electricity and gas in New Jersey. The mix of revenues is 31% residential, 45% commercial, 22% industrial. *Annual revenues: $4.9 billion.*

- Pacific Gas & Electric   S&P rating: A
  Current yields: 8.7% to 9.7%

Pacific Gas & Electric supplies electricity and gas to forty-eight counties in California. 72% of revenues are from electricity and 28% from sales of gas. The company has more than forty-five bond issues outstanding. *Annual revenues: $9+ billion.*

$$ ACTION TIP: Avoid buying bonds not listed on the New York Exchange because they are difficult to buy or sell in lots of less than $100,000. However, with bonds listed on the NYSE, you can buy as few as five bonds through most full-service and discount brokers. The average commission ranges from $5 to $7.50 per bond.

Although not everyone is game to put their money in the market, you can see that the recession offers a number of investment opportunities. Even so, bear in mind the soundest investment advice of all: Never put all of your eggs in one basket. Diversify your recession portfolio among some of these suggestions and safer choices as well, such as bank CDs, Treasury issues, and money market funds.

# 4

# Losing Your Job
# and Finding a New One

"YOU'RE fired." Those have to be the two most dreaded words in the world of work. Maybe it has already happened to you, or you're afraid that it will. Worrying about unemployment is an all too real fear these days. In recent years, American corporations have eliminated thousands of blue-collar, white-collar, and pinstripe jobs. No company, not even among the pillars of the corporate world, is immune to cutbacks. Men and women who expected to glide into retirement are cast adrift. Those on the fast track suddenly find themselves derailed. Younger employees, hoping to build their careers, are out pounding the pavements instead.

If you're one of the many men and women who have lost a job due to "downsizing" or "streamlining," you're facing many difficult decisions. At a time when keeping your wits about you is crucial, the emotional pain and financial turmoil caused by involuntary unemployment is likely to cause panic. It's natural to feel badly; it's counterproductive to panic. Remember that there are ways to reduce the pain and increase the likelihood of finding a new job. Think of this chapter as your survival guide: It will help you find a new job in a shrinking marketplace and get through the days until you're happily reemployed.

As you're reading this chapter, and while you're conducting a job search, keep in mind that being fired can actually be the first step toward a new life, a new direction and a new career. It was true for Grace Mirabella and it can be true for you. Ms. Mirabella was fired from her longtime position as editor in chief of *Vogue* magazine. Although it was an enormous shock, within a year she had founded her own dynamic and successful magazine for women, *Mirabella*.

## EMPLOYED BUT FEARFUL

If you're one of the lucky ones, you are currently employed. Still, there may be that nagging doubt that it's only a matter of time. You might be wondering how safe *is* your job? Knowing how to interpret the many warning signals can help you prepare for the future. The experts all agree on one key point: Develop your strategy now, even if your job seems secure, for the old cliché is right—it's much easier to get another job while you're still employed. And if you think layoffs are coming your way, start planning before the ax falls!

You can begin by talking with your family and getting your finances in shape (more on how to do this on page 84). Think about ways to make extra money and save it as your own private unemployment fund. Consider training and upgrading your skills and knowledge. Finally, don't just keep your ears open to a better situation, start looking for one!

## WARNING SIGNALS AT YOUR WORKPLACE

Begin planning for a change if there's:

- A general slump in your industry.
- An economic downturn in your geographical area.
- Your company has a pile of debt and little cash flow.

- Management has already offered early retirement buy-outs.
- There's a freezing hire.
- Bonuses have been eliminated.
- There's talk about merging with another firm that does the same kind of work or produces the same types of products as yours.
- You're not invited to meetings you used to attend regularly.
- Your boss (or his/her boss) has been fired.
- There's talk of moving the company to a less expensive location.

## HOW TO SAFEGUARD YOUR JOB

Layoffs can be fairly arbitrary. Often it is the most recently hired employees who are the first to be terminated; sometimes it's an entire division. But there are things you can do to make your boss or his/her boss think twice before giving you a pink slip. During a recession, it's more important than ever to:

- Get to work on time.
- Don't call in sick unless you are.
- Willingly and cheerfully assume new tasks or responsibilities.
- Accept reduced hours rather than quit.
- Suggest ways the company could save money or make more.
- Do your work carefully.

## YOU'RE NOT ALONE: DEALING WITH THE SHOCK

No matter how well-prepared you are, getting fired is traumatic. If it happens to you, there are some important guidelines to follow: First and foremost, don't feel ashamed and don't unleash your anger at your employer. You will be experiencing some powerful emotions and as you move through various and conflicting feelings, it will be helpful to remember the example of Grace Mirabella.

## DON'T HIDE

In today's economic climate there's no shame attached to losing a job. In one month alone (November 1990) unemployment hit 5.7%—that translated into 68,000 people getting the ax. So you're certainly not alone. And since you will need a wide support network to help you find a new job and to keep your spirits up, hiding the situation from family, friends, and potential employers is the worst thing you can do.

## STAY COOL

Getting that pink slip makes most people angry, and justifiably so, but don't let it show. The company has already made up its mind and the chances of getting them to change it are extremely slim. Restrain any urge to lash out and let management have it. You will only jeopardize your chances of getting a good referral. Keep cool: Get letters of recommendation quickly and ask for a follow-up meeting within a day or two to discuss the details of your severance package. Find out if the firm has an outplacement service—many companies pick up the cost of this counseling. (See the section on outplacement, page 96.) If the company offers to help you find a new job, don't be proud: It may have been years since you were last interviewed. If you were hired straight out of school, or have worked at only one or two places, your interview skills are probably rusty, and your resume may be out of date. You may even naively expect another company to take the initiative and ask you to work for them, in which case you've talked yourself out of learning how to research the job market. In today's recession, this is a big mistake. Let the firm that has fired you help you get up to snuff.

Being fired *always* comes as a great emotional shock—it's like being dumped in a bucket of ice water. You had a job when you woke up in the morning but by the time you went to bed, you were unemployed. Some have described the trauma as the equivalent of getting divorced or being in an earthquake. But resist the temptation to go around bad-mouthing the firm or your boss to other employees or people outside the firm—again, this only undermines a successful job search. And if you're given an exit interview, don't tell all. A negative report may affect your references. Forget about revenge and concentrate on the future.

## RECOGNIZING YOUR FEELINGS

Although it's counterproductive to let loose with certain emotions, especially at your former employer, it's equally foolish to bury them. The first step toward getting over the shock of losing your job is to recognize your emotional state. Don't be surprised if you feel:

- *Anger.* Many people become angry because they have been rejected by their employer. Anger is focused on the boss, the company, even one's family or oneself.
- *Depression.* The feeling of rejection can lead to depression.
- *Revenge.* Some people say, "I'm really going to show them." (You will; by keeping cool and getting another job.)
- *Vulnerable.* In order to get a new job, you must offer yourself to new people, exposing personal strengths, weaknesses, and hopes. And it means facing the possibility of rejection again.
- *Loneliness.* Some people won't stick by you when you're out of work. The loss of fair-weather friends can lead to a feeling of loneliness.
- *Self-doubt.* Very serious types may begin to doubt that they ever were competent, when in fact they have been doing excellent work for many years.
- *Embarrassment.* Being out of a job is no fun, but it is *not* a sign of failure either. However, some people feel extremely embarrassed, as if they are no longer a valuable member of their family or community.

At first you may be surprised at the depths of your feelings; you may even try to deny them. Yet knowing that many others share similar reactions is comforting. You can expect rapid mood swings, highs and lows, as you look for a new job. But if you have any of the feelings described in the box above for long periods of time, they will become counterproductive and will immobilize you. Therefore, it is important to focus on productive activities—primarily looking for new work.

## THE THREE STAGES OF RECOVERY

The first stage inevitably is one of both shock and denial. You are incredulous and wonder, "Why me?" This stage may last only a few days or it may last as long as a month or six weeks. The second stage, one of anger and depression, is the most debilitating since it's difficult, if not impossible, to interview well or even search effectively for a new position while weighed down by these feelings. If either stage persists for more than several weeks, seek help in moving on to the third and final stage, that of understanding and acceptance. This recovery process takes longer for some than others but when you hit the third and final phase, that of acceptance, you will be more successful in finding a new job.

If, after you pass through the three stages of recovery, you are still moody, depressed, or feeling hopeless, consult a professional, a psychiatrist or counselor who specializes in helping unemployed men and women recover their sense of self-worth and confidence.

## PAIN BRINGS GAIN

In many instances, being fired actually winds up being positive. Executives and managers who are fired from high-power, stressful jobs with large corporations often find greater job satisfaction working for smaller businesses where they have more say in decision-making. Balancing work life and family life is also easier in less-pressured positions. Those who start up their own business, pouring their heart and soul into making *their* company work, also find it more fulfilling than working for someone else.

## FINALLY, DON'T BLAME YOURSELF

Fired workers, especially professionals, tend to blame themselves for being let go, dredging up past mistakes rather than accepting that being fired is often a matter of economics rather than any serious personal faults.

## HOW YOUR FAMILY CAN HELP

If someone in your family loses their job, your response can either help or hinder their recovery. Being handed a pink slip can be completely devastating, shattering one's feelings of importance and productivity. Some of this damage can be repaired by a spouse or close friend letting the person know that "We love you for who you are, not for what you do."

As the spouse or friend of someone who has been fired, make it a point to keep up regular family activities and include the unemployed member just as before. Continue to go to the movies, on picnics, to visit family and friends, attend baseball games, PTA events, etc. Don't pooh-pooh that person's feelings. It may be tempting to say, "Don't worry. You're smart. I know you'll get another job soon." This type of statement belittles the powerful feelings that someone who is unemployed has. Instead, acknowledge that the situation is difficult and make it very clear that you care and will help. Finally, don't expect the person's energy level and enthusiasm to bound back the minute he or she returns to work. For some, healing is a slow process. Yet life doesn't have to end with the pink slip—it can be the start of something new and better.

# WHAT TO TELL THE CHILDREN

Children are typically frightened and confused when a parent loses a job. Yet if the situation is handled well, it can result in positive growth, with family members drawing closer to one another. Psychologists stress the importance of dealing openly and honestly with children. Hiding things only adds to their fears, since kids have a seemingly innate ability to see through lies and cover-ups. Concealment of the situation is not only harmful, it's futile. Instead, give them the simple facts and explain how you're going about looking for new work. Reassure them that life will go on, although there may be some changes, such as fewer gifts at Christmas, or day camp instead of sleep-away camp. The more concrete you can be in your discussion, the more secure children will feel with future changes. If you're not dining out much anymore or you're canceling the summer trip, tell them. They'll eventually know anyway.

It's also important to explain that the situation is temporary, although you don't know exactly how long it will take until you're working again. Reassure them that a recession is a cyclical thing, that good times and bad times come in cycles and eventually life will return to normal or near normal.

But be realistic. A child's confidence in his parent may be eroded, at least temporarily. That's why honesty on your part is so essential to preserving children's trust. Try to hide something from them and they simply imagine worse things going on. In fact, children often tend to blame themselves for problems that are not their fault. Very young children may feel responsible for their parent's distress unless the real reason is explained to them. Tell your children why you're upset and why you're home.

It also helps if you encourage your children to look on the bright side. You will be able to spend a lot more time with them. Avoid an atmosphere of continual pessimism—you want them to learn that difficulties can be overcome. It will also help if you don't show the full extent of your pain and worries—the degree to which you reveal your full feelings depends upon the age of your child and his or her resiliency in times of adversity. One can obviously be more open with a teenager or college student than with a five- or six-year-old.

If your child is worried, don't trivialize his feelings by saying something like, "Now what on earth are you upset about?" Instead, reassure him that his concern is natural. You might encourage him to take on some responsibility that's appropriate to his age and abilities, such as a paper route or a Saturday job. And finally, don't forget that your child's teachers can be extremely supportive. Let them know you're out of work so they can help your child if he has trouble at school or with other children.

$$ ACTION TIP: Consult *Parent Survival Training* by David A. Lustig and Marvin Silverman (North Hollywood, CA: Wilshire Book Co., 1988). The cost is $10.00.

## COPING WITH THE RECESSION BLUES

If you are suffering from the recession blues, you're not alone—anyone who tells you that he or she never feels down is fooling themselves. But the blues can be dealt with. The first step is to know something about emotions and how they work.

It's important to remember that, though you have some measure of control over your emotional response to a given situation, that control is far from complete. Even when everything is going well—the job, your family, your love life—there are probably still times when you feel curiously down and discouraged. When you lose a job or your income plummets, it's only natural for you to feel blue. But now the balance shifts. Instead of feeling good most of the time and depressed once in a while, you begin to feel depressed most of the time and cheerful only intermittently. The most common symptoms of recession blues are: 1) A lowered feeling of self-esteem; 2) pessimistic outlook; and 3) lack of interest in seeking pleasure of any kind, from bowling to sex.

## How to Cope

You can start to turn the situation around by recognizing that what you feel is perfectly justified and not due to any weakness on your part. If you *didn't* feel a little depressed when things go really wrong, you would neither be aware nor very realistic. So don't try to fight these "down" feelings every minute. Instead, try to relax. Sleep, watch TV, read, go to the movies, take a walk. Do whatever seems helpful. At first you'll have perhaps one good afternoon every few days, then a whole day, and after a while you will actually want to get up and out and do something about finding a new job.

Here are some healthy ways to fight the blues:

- Find friends who are also out of work and form a support group to take early morning walks. This will encourage you to get up and dressed in the morning.
- The same group can go together to collect unemployment checks, meet for breakfast, go to the library, etc.
- If you live alone, set up a life of alternatives. Having options is an enormous blues-fighter. At all times: Have two good books to read, a TV series to watch, a date for Saturday night dinner, and an activity for Sunday.
- Exercise regularly. Jogging, bicycle riding, fast walking, swimming are all great medicines for the blues.
- Don't blame yourself. Remember, Americans all over the country are being thrown out of work by the thousands.
- Don't drop out. You might think you're the only one in your crowd to whom this is happening. And maybe you are. Hang in there and stay active in your social group.
- Finally, if you are seriously depressed and don't seem to be able to bounce back, seek professional help. Your doctor, the director of social work at your hospital, or a knowl-

edgeable friend can refer you to a counselor or a psychiatrist. If these referral sources are not available to you, then call the National Mental Health Association Information Center, 800-969-NMHA. The group has 600 associations across the country that can make appropriate referrals for low cost counseling. Or, contact the National Federation of Societies for Clinical Social Work, Box 3740, Arlington, VA 22203, (703-522-3866) for the nearest society for referrals.

## FINANCES WHILE OUT OF WORK:
## A SURVIVAL GUIDE

You've been laid off, fired, axed—and now you must make some critical choices about what to do with retirement money, severance pay, medical coverage, and unemployment benefits. You're going to have to make a realistic budget—and stick to it. Don't panic, don't hide, and don't put off these decisions, no matter how tempting it is to deal with realities later. The decisions you make now will help alleviate a financial crunch in the weeks and months ahead. Get the facts and then act. Don't allow shock or feelings of vulnerability to prevent you from making the right moves.

The best place to start is at your old firm's benefits office. Your leverage with your old firm is greatest the day or two after you've been fired, while management is still feeling bad about letting you and others go. This is the time to ask for outplacement help (see page 96) and find out about other benefits.

The nine steps that follow should help you achieve a sound financial plan:

Step 1. *Severance pay.* Employees told to clean out their desks almost always receive a severance check. It may be enough to last one year, two weeks, or somewhere in between. Keep the severance money in something liquid—a money market account at your bank or a money market mutual fund. The latter pay higher rates. (For a list of top-yielding money funds see page 30.) If you receive a sizable amount, put half in a six-month or one-year CD and half in a money fund. Use the portion in the money fund to cover short-term expenses. If you are given the choice of taking severance in a lump sum or in payments, it's generally best to opt for the lump sum and invest it so it starts earning interest. If you do this you won't need to worry about your ex-employer's financial health. If it's near year-end, however, you might want to schedule payments so you can defer income to the next year. (Severance money is taxable in the year received.)

$$ ACTION TIP: A common reaction and mistake is to use the severance check (or lump-sum payouts from a retirement plan) to pay off the mortgage. If you need liquidity, this is a major mistake. A mortgage is often one of the lowest-rate loans and interest is tax-deductible.

Step 2. *Retirement money.* If you receive a large sum from your 401(k) plan or other retirement plan, try not to touch it. That money has never been taxed and if you take it out now, you will pay income taxes on it plus a 10% penalty if you're under age fifty-nine and a half. Most 401(k) plans allow former employees to keep their money invested with the former employer as long as they like. In many cases, profit-sharing and stock option plans can also be left with your company. If your former company should go bankrupt, you will still be protected since pension plans do not fall into bankruptcy proceedings. However, if a pension fund is under-funded, you could be out of luck. If you have any suspicions about the security of your pension, take it with you. If you opt to take it with you or you're not allowed to leave your money with your firm, roll it over into an IRA with a mutual fund, bank, or brokerage firm. As long as you don't spend it, it will continue to grow on a tax-deferred basis with no penalties involved. Sometimes circumstances will force you to withdraw some of your retirement funds (see Step 8).

Step 3. *Begin preparing for leaner times.* Avert real financial disaster by sharpening your pencil and drawing up a budget to deal with the loss of a regular paycheck. Although the old rule about job hunting—that one month of searching is needed for each $10,000 of salary desired—may not be completely accurate, use it as a guideline for lean-time budgeting. (See pages 22–26 for a budget worksheet.)

For your crisis budget:

a) *List those bills which you absolutely must pay,* such as mortgage or rent, insurance, car loan, gasoline, food, telephone, electricity, and the cost of looking for another job.

b) *List all items you can reduce or cut out completely,* such as eating out, travel, vacations, new car, and new clothes. By reining in consumption urges, you'll discover what your real needs are.

c) *Leave the plastic at home.* Paying for items with cash or a check curbs impulse purchases and helps you "feel" the money going out.

Step 4. *Slowly tap assets* if necessary. Begin with savings, money market funds, CDs, stocks, and bonds. Avoid touching your retirement plan, IRA, Keogh, SEP, 401(k). Instead, sell that extra car or other luxury items.

Step 5. *Write to the head of the credit department* of those creditors not in your "must pay" file, informing them that you'll be sending them "good faith" checks until you are employed again. Let them know how much they can expect —$50, $100, or $250 a month. If you're still coming up short, talk to your mortgage lender (preferably in person) and try to negotiate smaller payments or a grace period until you find a new job. Most banks prefer cash to foreclosure.

Step 6. *Maximize income.* After trimming expenditures, look for other sources of income. Depending on your portfolio, sell growth stocks and buy income-producing bonds, liquidate other assets, or borrow. (See page 121 on savvy borrowing techniques.) Remember, once assets are sold, they're hard to replace or rebuild, so it might be wise to first borrow against securities, life insurance policies, or even your home. (See pages 133–135.) (It's best to refinance your house before you're actually unemployed.)

Step 7. *Don't be too proud to take unemployment insurance* if you were fired. (You cannot collect unemployment income if you leave voluntarily.) You and your employer have helped fund this benefit over the years; you're entitled to use it. (See the section on unemployment insurance on page 89.)

Step 8. *In a true emergency* you may have to use some of your retirement savings. Use the rolled-over funds that are in an IRA, or use money in an existing IRA. Put it in a money market fund if it's not there already and write checks only when absolutely necessary and after all other severance and savings are gone. NOTE: You'll pay income taxes (and a 10% penalty if under age 59 ½) on this money as you dip into it. In some cases borrowing is a better short-term solution; see Chapter 5.

Step 9. *Keep track of job-hunting expenses*. It costs money to look for a job and some of these expenses may be deducted from your taxable income as "miscellaneous itemized deductions." However, the IRS rules are somewhat complicated, so check with an accountant. In general, the total amount of deductions must exceed 2% of your adjusted gross income and they must be spent in search of a job in the same line of work. You don't actually have to find a new job to take the deductions. But, if you are unemployed, the IRS may disallow the deductions if it finds you took too much time between your past job and starting to look for a new one—it does not define what too much time is. So keep all receipts and write on each one the date, the purpose, and the person or company contacted. Among the expenses to track are: recruitment and agency fees, transportation, telephone calls and resumé preparation.

When you take a look at your budget, you will probably find several expenses you can eliminate—health care is not one of them! No matter how healthy you are, all it takes is one medical emergency to wipe out your savings. The good news is that the majority of people have several options they can pursue.

In 1986 a federal law was enacted requiring that employers (provided the company has over twenty employees) sponsoring group health plans offer their employees and their dependents the opportunity to extend their health coverage at group rates. This is called "continuation coverage." Under the law, you have sixty days from the date you would lose coverage to apply for continuation coverage. (Within fourteen days of your termination, the employer must provide you with the proper paperwork to apply for such coverage.) If you choose continuation coverage, the company is required to give you the identical coverage provided under the group plan.

Continuation coverage lasts for eighteen months (longer if you are disabled). You do not have to show that you are insurable to choose continuation coverage. The insurance company must keep you on, regardless of your health situation or history—in other words, coverage must continue even if you have a preexisting condition. This is invaluable for someone with a serious illness.

It is essential to hold on to health insurance coverage while between jobs, yet insurance is usually more expensive than people realize. Employees usually pay only a small portion of group rate coverage, if any at all, and when they lose their jobs they must pay all of the costs for continuation coverage, plus an additional 2% service charge if the employer wishes to levy this fee. (You also must make timely payments or you can be dropped from the plan.) If you worked for a company or business that shut down and the plan is dropped, there usually is no continuation coverage.

Here are some additional tips from the National Insurance Consumers Organization (NICO) to help you maintain adequate coverage:

- If you're self-employed, look into membership in the National Association for the Self-Employed which will make you eligible for its group plan. Contact the Association at 817-589-2475 or 800-232-NASE. Membership is $48.

- If you are forced into purchasing an individual policy, check the *National Underwriter* at your library. This trade publication has an annual *Life and Health issue with an "Individual Leaders List"* of the 250 companies that sell the largest volume nationwide. The cost is $4; to order call 800-543-0874.

- Ask about special group rates offered by professional associations, unions, or an alumni association.

- For information on health maintenance organizations (HMOs), their standard policies, and where to find the best deals, send $3 and a stamped, self-addressed envelope to: NICO, 121 North Payne Street, Alexandria, VA 22314, or call 703-549-8050. Ask for a copy of "Buyers' Guide to Insurance."

## EVERYTHING YOU NEED TO KNOW ABOUT UNEMPLOYMENT INSURANCE

In 1989, only about one-third of the 6.5 million Americans out of work collected unemployment benefits. That statistic is down from a 1975 high of 75%. The Urban Institute reports that this low percentage is partially due to the fact that many jobless people fail to apply, believing they're not eligible for benefits.

It's true that there is some confusion regarding unemployment insurance. The benefits, and duration for which they are paid, vary widely between the states. Most states tie benefits to the amount of wages you last earned and the length of time worked for your last employer. Longtime employees typically get twenty-six weeks of benefits. As of late 1990, the weekly maximums ranged from $134 in Nebraska to $408 in Massachusetts. In New York, you receive 50% of gross income, up to a ceiling of $260 a week. The date payments start varies, too. They can begin one week after being terminated, or after the period covered by severance pay, or after the value of unused vacations and holidays are used up.

Regardless of where you live, over the years part of your salary has gone into funding unemployment insurance. You are now entitled to get some of that money back. Don't let embarrassment—or confusion—prevent you from getting the help you deserve.

*Apply at once:* Apply by filing your claim immediately after your last day of work. Most people are eligible for only six months of unemployment insurance, so if you don't apply immediately and you get a job before the end of the six months, you lose those payments.

*Where to apply:* Check your telephone directory under the State Government section. You will find it listed under Employment Development Department, Employee Assistance, or Unemployment Insurance Claims. Then call the nearest office and find out the hours. You will need to make an appointment to file your claim.

*You will need:* A pen, your social security number, previous employer's name and address, your job title, and reason for leaving. Don't lie. The interviewer checks everything with your former employer.

*Miscellaneous hints:* Be on time for your appointment. Wear your normal business clothes, not only to make a positive impression on the interviewer but also to help you maintain a feeling of self-worth. If for some reason you are treated unkindly or rudely, try not to react. Lines are long, so bring something to read.

Most states require that you show proof of your efforts to get a job—this often means keeping a log of interviews with telephone numbers and copies of letters to prospective employers. You are required to look for a job in your field or a related one.

*Taxes:* All unemployment compensation benefits must be included in your annual taxable gross income. Keep records of all checks you receive, even though you will receive a 1099 form.

## FINDING A NEW JOB

There are any number of proven ways to land a new job, from reading the want ads to starting your own business. Use as many of the following suggestions as possible and you will increase your success ratio and decrease your search time. Since 85% of the jobs available are not advertised, your first step should be to network. It is the single most effective job search technique, especially for nonunion positions. But before your start contacting others, it's helpful to study your own skills, contributions, and talents—you may discover some you never used before and other you had neglected. This will help you in directing your search, preparing your resumé, fine tuning your interview skills, and keeping up your spirits.

## RECOGNIZING YOUR TALENTS

Being let go provides an excellent opportunity to reconsider what to do with the rest of your life and whether you're in the right type of work. Ask yourself: What do I really like to do? What am I really good at? Simplistic as these questions may sound, take the time to write down your thoughts on paper. Discuss your likes and dislikes with someone who knows you well.

If you do decide to change directions, make the switch into

doing something that you like. Wally Amos, who was a Los Angeles talent scout, left show biz to open a chocolate chip cookie store in the mid-1970s. Some people thought he was crazy, but he had always loved his Aunt Della's cookies. He figured other people would, too. And they did: Five years later, Famous Amos cookies were a national success, bringing in more than $5 million a year!

Before you make any change, take some time to focus on your skills. Many of us are either too general or too narrow when selling our skills to a prospective employer, probably because we haven't given them a great deal of consideration. Once you are fully aware of your strengths and abilities, you should be able to define yourself in those terms. Then you can relate your particular skills to an employer's needs.

$$ ACTION TIP: Read *The Outplacement Solution: Getting the Right Job After Mergers, Takeovers, Layoffs, and Other Corporate Chaos* by Karen S. Wolfer and Richard G. Wong (New York: John Wiley & Sons, Inc., 1988; $12.95). This book has many useful worksheets and ideas for discovering the real working you.

# YOUR PROVEN JOB STRENGTHS

Put a checkmark next to those strengths which you posses. It will help you select a new area of work as well as boost your self-confidence when you see how many things you do well.

_____ on time
_____ seldom absent
_____ decision-maker
_____ excellent writer
_____ a team player
_____ like details
_____ good with numbers
_____ good business sense
_____ accurate
_____ a self-starter
_____ good researcher
_____ committed
_____ cooperative
_____ well-organized
_____ supportive of others
_____ follow through
_____ instruct well
_____ take initiative
_____ face difficulties
_____ make good suggestions
_____ motivate others
_____ assume responsibilities
_____ efficient
_____ hard worker
_____ record of stability
_____ competent in my field

_____ good speaker
_____ precise
_____ global thinker
_____ analytical mind
_____ can work alone/independently
_____ administrative ability
_____ learn quickly
_____ inventive problem-solver
_____ honest
_____ enterprising
_____ quality oriented
_____ delegate well
_____ communicate well
_____ adaptable
_____ mechanically skilled
_____ productive
_____ can correct others
_____ like new challenges
_____ follow directions
_____ other:
_____
_____
_____
_____

## YOUR RESUMÉ

Most of the information you need to put together an effective resumé can be found in *What Color Is Your Parachute?* by Richard Nelson Bolles (Berkeley: Ten Speed Press, 1991; $11.95). But as you prepare your resumé, keep these guidelines in mind:

1. A resumé is a supplement to the interview, not a substitute.
2. People get hired most often because of personal chemistry, not their resumé or other paperwork. (The possible exception is writers.)
3. Try to precede your resumé with a phone call and always leave a copy behind after an interview for your interviewer to study.
4. Don't reveal everything in the resumé; leave some things to be discussed in a face-to-face interview. Bring up "extras" in person, such as awards, honors, languages, hobbies, etc.
5. Summarize any work that took place more than ten years ago under "Early Experience."
6. <u>Don't include age, sex, national origin, race, religion or political affiliation, hobbies, salary history or requirements, reasons for leaving previous position, or your photograph</u>.
7. Keep it short—one page should do; *never* go over two pages.

## NETWORKING

Networking—the art of talking to friends, acquaintances, and everyone you know without directly asking them for a job—is a particularly important way to find a job during hard times. Although there are jobs available, they may take longer to land because many corporations cut the cost of advertising for jobs when the economy slows down. Most positions never appear in the help-wanted ads. Networking is a social process with a business purpose, building a chain of contacts between you and the business that needs you. By keeping in touch with people you know, you will find the names of other people they know who could give you information, ideas, and contacts to help you land a job.

**$$ ACTION TIP**: Begin by telling your friends and acquaintances that you're looking for work. Make a list of your contacts—try to build up to 100 and eventually 200. Start contacting those who are easiest for you to call.

## NETWORKING CATEGORIES

Friends, relatives, colleagues
Neighbors
Professional and trade
   associations
Politicians/civic leaders
Business owners/merchants
Librarians
Newspaper people
Financial planner/stockbroker
Travel acquaintances
Children's teachers
Competitors
Address book/Rolodex

Coworkers, past and present
Doctors/dentists/lawyers/
   accountants/bankers
Clergy
Club and church members
Retirees
Fund-raisers
Real estate brokers
Consultants
Fraternities/Sororities
Military service
Chamber of Commerce
Volunteer organizations

Get a copy of your school alumni directory, and send letters to all those in your field. Explain that you're looking for contacts and you'll follow up with a phone call. Enclose your resumé. Eventually you'll hear from someone who either has a job or knows of someone who does.

*Networking hints.* In order for networking to be effective:

1. Know what type of work you want.
2. If you know the neighborhood in which you want to

work, find people who work in that area. Ask them about job opportunities, new plant openings, new divisions being formed at an existing company.

3. Prepare ahead of time before calling contacts. Decide if you're looking for advice or other contacts in the field. Write down the points you want to make.

4. If you are contacting a stranger, write first and then follow up with a phone call. Always try to set up a personal meeting.

5. When you do meet, remember that it's not a job interview. The purpose of the meeting is to gather information related to your job objective. Take notes. Ask for contacts after some conversation. Ask for the person's business card and leave your calling card.

6. Write a thank-you note. Later on, write again to let them know how your search is going and remind them you're still looking. (When you are reemployed, write again to let them know!)

## OUTPLACEMENT

Unlike an employment agency, an outplacement firm will not find you a job, but it will help you prepare for looking for one, and to determine what kind of job you're best suited for. This service, which initially provided help for top-level managers, lawyers, and other professionals on an individual basis, is now being offered to less high-level employees. One of the first questions you should ask when you are fired is "Do I get outplacement help?" If the answer is yes, then the company pays the bill.

Outplacement firms may provide:

- Individual counseling sessions, often with a psychologist.
- An assessment of your achievements and skills which leads to setting career and salary goals.

- Seminars at which job-search techniques are taught; help in resumé-writing is given along with a refresher course on interviewing techniques.
- The right to use the outplacement firm's clerical help, telephone, and office space while searching for a job.
- Specific suggestions for where to look for work.

Perhaps most importantly, you will be with other people in the same boat; you'll receive moral support as well as peer pressure to start taking action.

$$ ACTION TIP: Read *The 1990–1991 Directory of Outplacement Firms* (Fitzwilliam, NH: Kennedy Publications; $69.95), available in larger libraries.

### Alternatives to Outplacement Firms

Try calling local university placement offices and ask for names of competent job-search counselors who do private consultation. Or check your local Y; many have helpful programs for those out of work. Another less expensive source is the 40-Plus Clubs. These self-help groups for unemployed managers, executives, and professionals over the age of forty provide training, office space, telephones, and support groups. Although the entrance fee is nominal, generally you must devote at least one day a week to helping other members locate jobs. There are 40-Plus Clubs in most major cities. Check your phone book or call the national headquarters (212-233-6086) for the club closest to you.

## DIRECT CONTACT WITH COMPANIES

Send cover letters and resumés to the specific companies you would like to work for. Generally, it's best not to send your resumé to the personnel department; instead you should go directly to the person responsible for hiring in the division or department you're interested in. Always follow up with a phone call to set up a personal interview.

Even if you don't get the job, never take "no" as a permanent "no"—at least not right away. Answer a rejection letter in writing, letting the individual know that you're disappointed, that you're still interested, and that you will contact them in a month or six weeks in case another job comes up. CAUTION: Don't be a pest. Call only once a month.

## EXECUTIVE RECRUITERS

If you're seeking an executive position, you certainly can contact executive search firms. They are hired by a company when it has a specific opening to fill. Some recruiters will accept resumés from individuals and keep them on file for future openings, but you should be aware that they receive hundreds of resumés each week and usually are filling only a handful of top positions.

$$ ACTION TIP: Consult *The 1991 Directory of Executive Recruiters* (Fitzwilliam, NH: Kennedy Publications; $39.95), available at larger libraries and outplacement firms.

## EMPLOYMENT AGENCIES AND WANT ADS

Register with agencies that handle the type of work you're interested in, and answer any ad that you find of interest. In addition to the newspaper, check those in magazines and trade publications. Get a jump on the competition: The Sunday *New York Times* employment section is usually available several days earlier. Call to find out how you can get it before Sunday. And have trade magazines sent to you by overnight mail.

$$ ACTION TIP: Most public libraries have job placement centers where you will find material on how to get work as well as lists of government agencies and companies seeking workers in the area.

# KEEPING UP YOUR SPIRITS AND SELF-IMAGE

Whether or not you use an outplacement firm, a recruiter, or an employment agency, you still have to do much of the work yourself. Begin with a careful, detailed review of your options. List your major career accomplishments, your particular skills, your income goals, and where you would like or be willing to live. Be prepared for a cool reception—you will probably be told "no" again and again. Keeping up your morale is essential to landing a job. To do this:

1. Get up at your regular time; don't sleep late.
2. Dress as if you were going to work; get out of your bathrobe.
3. Keep up contacts: Play in your regular golf, tennis, or bowling game; attend dinner with friends; play bridge; go to the movies.
4. Lose weight if you need to.
5. Keep your hair cut and your shoes polished.

# THE BIG MOMENT: INTERVIEW HINTS

It is essential that you thoroughly prepare for all job interviews. *Before the interview*, do your homework. Go to the library and read corporation write-ups in Standard & Poor's or *Value Line* if it is a public company. For both public and private firms, get the most recent annual report, talk to people in the community, and, if possible, the company's customers and suppliers. Then mentally review your top five skills and strengths. Rehearse your conversation, ideally in front of a mirror or video camera. Get to the interview fifteen minutes ahead of time so you can familiarize yourself with the surroundings and relax.

*During the interview*, listen, ask appropriate questions, make eye contact, smile, and be yourself.

The typical questions you can expect in an interview are:

1. Tell me about yourself.
2. What did you accomplish in your job at _____ ?
3. Why did you leave?
4. What were some of the more challenging things you did in your last job?
5. Describe your last boss/manager/supervisor.
6. Why should we hire you?
7. What are your interests outside of work?
8. Where do you want to be five years from now?
9. Why do you want to work for us?
10. What are your salary expectations?

To the toughest question, why did you leave, simply state, "There was a takeover [or "a reorganization"]. You do not need to elaborate. Use the past as a springboard to the present; in other words, use active verbs: "I *worked* on this project," not "I used to work on . . ."

*Body language* is essential to your success. Don't posture and make yourself look silly, but do sit forward when the interviewer is speaking and be genuinely interested. Watch the interviewer carefully. If he or she starts to fidget, wrap up your story.


## EMPLOYMENT CONTRACTS

When you do land a new job, ask for an employment contract—you may just get one. Many companies write such contracts to hold on to top employees because there's far less loyalty on the part of workers to companies than was the case in the past. Gone are the days when employees worked all their lives for the same business. The typical contract covers compensation, bonus, benefits, perks, and termination.

Some specifics to check are: 1) that the contract provides very specific protection—not just general employment with the company but your particular job or position; 2) that all aspects of compensation are really clear, including salary, annual bonus, and retirement package; 3) that you can use the American Arbitration Association for settling disputes rather than a court, which is usually more expensive, and that your legal fees will be covered. Steer clear of a noncomplete clause which limits your freedom to take a job with a direct competitor.

## WHERE THE JOBS ARE

Looking down the line, the Bureau of Labor Statistics estimates that by the year 2000, professionals in these fields will be in great demand: engineers, computer experts, doctors, health scientists, lawyers, and teachers. More than four in ten jobs (about seven million new jobs will be created by the year 2000) will be technical, administrative, or professional. People with technical knowledge combined with knowledge of accounting principles, finance, and marketing will be most sought after.

For a listing of industries that typically thrive during a recession, see pages 59–60.

$$ ACTION TIP: If you're looking for employment now, check your local phone books for firms such as Mail Boxes and Mail Room Etc. which wrap and mail items.

## WHERE THE JOBS AREN'T

In general, the following industries suffer during recessionary periods:

• Retail stores
• Some manufacturing

- Autos and auto sales
- Public relations
- Advertising
- Human resources
- Government jobs
- Construction

Of course, there will always be job openings in these areas, but you can expect a lot of competition. Don't give up, but you might want to consider some of the alternatives below in the meantime.

## FREE-LANCING, CONSULTING, MOONLIGHTING, AND TEMPING

If you like and are good at what you're doing, it's possible to keep on doing it by consulting or free-lancing. Or you might take any job just to earn money, doing it on the side (commonly known as moonlighting). Before setting your fees, check with other free-lancers or call several employment agencies to determine the going rates in your field and geographical area. Most beginning free-lancers undervalue their talent and time. Check your yellow pages for free-lance networks or associations.

Most people have many more skills than they are aware of. Review this list and select those that interest you. You can find free-lance work by word of mouth; advertising in newspapers, trade journals, and association newsletters; or, depending on where you live, by putting a flyer or your business card on community and office bulletin boards. And don't forget about temporary employment agencies which will find work for you. A recession is an excellent time for free-lancers because so many businesses cut back on full-time employees.

## VALUABLE SKILLS FOR FREE-LANCERS

- Word Processing
- Secretarial work
- Accounting
- Writing
- Commercial art and design
- Financial planning
- Substitute teaching
- Care of elderly or ill
- Editorial work
- Tax preparation
- Photography
- Newsletter publishing
- Construction/home repairs
- Tutoring
- Child care
- Physical therapy

## CITIES TO EXPLORE

The tension in city halls throughout the country is at an all-time high as municipalities struggle against huge budget deficits, eroding tax bases, and rising unemployment. But not all the news on the urban front is gloom and doom. A number of cities have retooled and reinvigorated their economies. There's no guarantee that they will stay that way, but if you're thinking of relocating, here's what you should know.

- *Minneapolis*. Minnesota's largest city is the center of information-processing for a number of high-tech firms, including Cray Research and Honeywell. Health care, a recession-resistant business, is the city's number-one employer, surpassing agriculture. Farm product sales are strong, aided by the weaker dollar. The city's per capita debt (the total municipal debt divided by the number of citizens) is low: $655 and the budget is strong enough to grant the city's bonds and AAA rating.

- *Indianapolis*. The 60,000-seat Hoosier Dome has turned this city into the amateur sports capital of the country. Over the past six years some sixty hotels have been built.

Health, medical, and business services industries provide most of the new jobs. The city puts 5% of its money into a trust fund each year to finance public employee pension liabilities.

- *Portland, Oregon.* This city is benefitting from the globalization of the U.S. economy, especially trade and investments with Japan and other Pacific Rim countries. Since the NEC Corporation built an electronics plant there in the mid-1980s, some twenty other Japanese companies have settled in the area. Its debt load is light: $980 per capita.

- *Houston.* Although the city's economy is still fueled by energy, it is much more diversified than it was when oil prices collapsed in 1986. New growth areas are electronics, health care, biotechnology, and aerospace. In 1989, the city reported a surplus of $79 million.

---

## SEVENTEEN BRIGHT SPOTS

Cities expected to have a growing need for workers, as measured by help-wanted ads:

| | |
|---|---|
| Albuquerque, NM | Madison, WI |
| Corpus Christi, TX | Miami, FL |
| Grand Rapids, MI | Milwaukee, WI |
| Harrisburg, PA | New Orleans, LA |
| Houston, TX | Reno, NV |
| Indianapolis, IN | Sacramento, CA |
| Knoxville, TN | San Antonio, TX |
| Las Vegas, NV | Seattle, WA |

Tulsa, OK

---

## HOT SPOTS THROUGH THE YEAR 2000

According to a Commerce Department study, these cities will have the hottest economies through the nineties:

Anaheim, CA
Boise City, ID
Bradenton, FL
Colorado Springs, CO
Daytona Beach, FL
Ft. Collins, CO
Ft. Myers, FL
Ft. Walton Beach, FL
Las Vegas, NV
Melbourne, FL
Modesto, CA
Naples, FL
Nashville, TN
Ocala, FL
Olympia, WA
Orlando, FL
Panama City, FL

Phoenix, AZ
Provo, UT
Reno, NV
Riverside, CA
Sacramento, CA
Salt Lake City, UT
San Diego, CA
Santa Cruz, CA
Santa Fe, NM
Santa Rosa, CA
Sarasota, FL
Seattle, WA
Springfield, MO
Tallahassee, FL
Tampa - St. Pete, FL
Tuscon, AZ
Vancouver, WA

West Palm Beach, FL

## TIPS FOR OLDER WORKERS

Older workers often face subtle age discrimination as many companies prefer younger employees—not only can they can pay younger people less, but they can train them for specific tasks or positions. The good news is that there are fewer young people to enter the job market, and this demographic trend should slow down the "forced" retirement of older workers. What should you do if you are offered a so-called "voluntary" early retirement program?

## THE GOLDEN BOOT

Early-retirement and voluntary separation incentive packages are generally take-it-or-leave-it deals. A cash incentive, based upon age and the number of years with the firm, is dangled in front of you. Because the offer is made in an economically troubled environment, the time given for making up one's mind is often painfully short—usually a month to ninety days.

There are several points to weigh:

1. *Do you really have a choice?* If the offer has included a number of people, then you have not been singled out to leave. But if the company is trimming the fat and you elect to stay, will your position be the same or will your job and your compensation be less?

2. *If you decide to retire, can you maintain your life-style —or close to it?* Do you have enough in retirement income and other assets to keep you going? If not, you may be better off to keep working in order to build up retirement resources.

3. *How generous is the offer?* Workers under age fifty can expect a cash incentive of one week's to one month's salary per year of service. Executives over fifty should look for better deals. Find out what other companies have offered before accepting. Some will continue medical insurance and offer monthly payments until Social Security benefits kick in.

4. *Are you prepared psychologically for retirement?* If you close your briefcase before you had planned to, you'll not only lose money but you'll also be without the structure that for years has been a major part of your life. How will you feel about being cut adrift? If you love work, consider whether you can work part-time; ask if you can become a consultant for your old firm or a competitor.

You might also think about starting your own business (see page 110). Do you have enough capital to last until the business becomes profitable? Can you still live comfortably if the business fails and you lose your capital? Are you healthy enough to put in long hours of hard work?

## KNOW YOUR RIGHTS

The Older Workers Benefit Protection Act, which amends the Age Discrimination in Employment Act, was signed into law on October 16, 1990. Its aim: To prohibit employers from reducing benefits because of an employee's age. Some of the provisions became effective at once while others will be phased in. The key rule is that benefit payments or costs incurred for an older worker cannot be less than those for a younger worker. In the past, some companies have tried to provide larger severance payments for younger workers and smaller payments for older workers, the rationale being that the older workers will be getting a pension. Under the new law, employers are prohibited from reducing or denying severance benefits for older workers simply because they are eligible for retirement. *Exception:* If severance benefits are payable because of a contingent event, such as a plant shutdown, they can be reduced by the value of "pension sweeteners." These are extra pension benefits related to the shutdown or other contingent event. This exception applies only if the employee is entitled to a full and immediate pension.

## FINDING WORK

If you do decide to retire, you can indeed find interesting work, although it may take some time and effort. When you talk to potential employers, begin by stressing your experience and indicate that money is not your key consideration. Keep age out of your resume. Target smaller and midsize companies that value experience rather than large companies that often prefer younger workers.

Certain employers seek out mature workers, realizing that they have valuable experience and are extremely reliable. Among the industries hiring senior employees are banking, hotels, travel, and temp agencies. And travel agencies, knowing that one in four trips is taken by someone age fifty-five or older, find the gray-haired employee a definite plus.

$$ ACTION TIPS: 1. Take a six- to eight-week course at a travel agent school; then enjoy the extra perks that come with the job, including reduced hotel rates and air-fares.

2. Try temping. Kelly Services, which has 850 offices in the U.S. and Canada, places older workers in all types of jobs. Adia and Volt agencies also place employees over age fifty-five.

3. Days Inn, Marriott, and other hotel and motel chains hire many older workers.

4. Be a seasonal tax helper. Demand for tax preparers and office workers is up during the first quarter of the year as people file their income tax returns. H&R Block offers a thirteen-week training course in the fall for $200. Completing the course does not guarantee a job, but it will help you pass the qualifying exam.

The IRS hires some 2,000 temporary workers to answer taxpayers' questions each year. Pay for this seasonal work, for which the IRS will train you, starts at about $14,500. In addition, the IRS hires 30,000 temps for its ten service centers. Salaries start at about $11,300. Call your local IRS office for details.

5. Contact the Senior Career Planning & Placement Service, which places retired executives in full- and part-time jobs across the country. To get details write or call 257 Park Avenue South, New York, NY 10010; 212-529-6660.

6. Contact Operation ABLE, an umbrella agency for senior employment programs around the country that help

people over fifty locate work. Their offices in eight cities have telephone hot lines for job search assistance. Call or write to: Operation ABLE, 180 North Wabash Avenue, Suite 802, Chicago, IL 60601; 312-782-3335.

7. The American Association of Retired Persons operates local workshops to help retirees looking for work. Contact AARP, 1909 K Street, NW, Washington, DC 20049, (202-872-4700) for the program in your area. For the free booklet "Working Options," send a postcard to the AARP Fulfillment Center at the same address.

8. The National Council on Aging tracks local employment agencies for older workers through its Senior Community Service Employment Program. Contact the Council at 600 Maryland Avenue, SW, Washington, DC 20024; 202-479-1200, or contact your state office on aging, listed in the blue pages of the phone book under "Aging."

Keep in mind that *Social Security benefits* are cut when annual wages are over $6,840 for those under age sixty-five, or $9,360 for those age sixty-five to sixty-nine. These dollar caps are periodically changed; for current figures call the IRS. If you are seventy, there is no limit. If your annual income tops these amounts, Social Security withholds $1 in benefits for every $2 of earnings above the limits. However, by working as a temp, when your income hits the cap, you can simply delay going to work until the next year.

You should also check up on the benefits you're entitled to receive from Social Security, whether you're planning on taking it now or years from now. Each year there are mistakes in 1 to 2% of the earnings data reported by employers to the Social Security Administration. Your entire earnings history determines the size of your retirement benefits, so it pays to check.

$$ ACTION TIP: Call 800-234-5772 and ask for Form 7004, "Request for Earnings and Benefit Estimate Statement." Include the age at which you plan to retire and the

average amount you expect to earn between now and then. The Social Security Administration will estimate your retirement benefit.

## STARTING A BUSINESS

Out-of-work men and women often start their own business or buy a franchise. But before sinking your savings into a small business, talk to others who have followed the entrepreneurial route. It can be lonely, risky, and hard work. According to the National Association for the Self-Employed, small business owners work an average of 52.5 hours per week, while other Americans work 43.5 hours.

It's not necessary to come up with a brilliant invention to go into your own business. What you must do, however, is do your job well . . . better than anyone else. Ray Kroc, who founded McDonald's did not invent the hamburger, but he did come up with a more efficient way to package and deliver it to Americans everywhere. McDonald's gives customers the old standard hamburger fast, cheaply, and in clean surroundings. That's why McDonald's is a success, not because the product was new. It's best to stick to a field you know and then carve out a special niche.

## BEFORE YOU BEGIN

New entrepreneurs face both joys and problems when they strike out on their own. The chances for more joys than headaches is enhanced if these realities are considered first:

1. *Take care of personal financial needs.* No one should begin a business if there's any question about where the money will come from for the mortgage or dinner next week — or even in the upcoming months. You should have enough cash saved to cover eighteen months of personal

expenses *above and beyond* the capital needed to launch the business.

2. *Take care of medical and disability insurance.* Most employees do not realize that benefits, such as life, health, and disability insurance, plus vacations and holidays, make up nearly one-third of their annual salary. To stay even, a new business must generate considerably more money than your old salary.

---

## SEVEN GOOD REASONS TO OWN A BUSINESS DURING HARD TIMES

Although the economy may be dropping and disposable income shrinking, smart entrepreneurs seize golden opportunities from the economic downturn. Here are the plusses of being a small business owner:

* Rents are down in many areas of the country.
* Free rent periods and other discounts are often negotiable.
* Cost of property is lower, making expansion feasible.
* More talented workers are seeking jobs.
* New employees can be hired for less than when times are good.
* The pie is getting smaller so well-run companies get more of the business that's out there.
* Discounts can be negotiated with suppliers.

---

## TURNING A HOBBY INTO A BUSINESS

As you look around, you will see people making money doing what once might have been their hobby: catering, teaching, collecting and selling antiques, etc. If you have a hobby, it may be relatively easy to turn it into a paying job. In fact, one of the ingredients for a successful start-up business is knowledge of the activity and in this respect, a hobbyist-turned-entrepreneur has a jump on the competition. And, if the new business can be run from home, it eliminates a significant expense—leasing space.

Instead of actually starting up a business, you could turn your hobby into full- or part-time work with someone else. For instance, if you like to arrange flowers, you could work at a florist's. If you enjoy working with computer spreadsheets, your friends or a local accounting firm might hire you as a tax preparer.

If you decide, however, to launch your own business, the nuts and bolts are the same as with any other operation. But, for purposes of deducting the costs (and any losses) on your federal income tax return, you must make a profit in three out of five consecutive years. The exception to this rule is horse breeding, training, racing, or showing, in which case there must be a profit in two of seven consecutive years.

## RAISING CAPTIAL

One of the biggest problems is finding the money to get started, since banks and venture capitalists seldom invest in a business until it has a proven track record. You may be able to find start-up money by tapping friends, relatives, partners, suppliers, and your own savings. Before knocking on doors, however, prepare a solid business plan—a walk-through on paper of everything an investor or lender needs to know about the business. Include a description of the venture, service, or product and what it will do, how it will be marketed and distributed, the problems it solves or voids in the marketplace it fills, the potential market, how many employees there will be, start-up expenses, estimated ongoing expenses for one year, other sources of money, a list of competitors, and, finally, an analysis of the risks involved.

**$$ ACTION TIP:** For help in preparing a business plan, check the phone book for the nearest office of SCORE, Service Corps of Retired Executives, or call the Small Business Administration (SBA) at 800-346-1614. SCORE is a division of the SBA. Women can gain help from AWED, 60 East 42nd Street, New York, NY 10165; 212-692-9100, 800-222-AWED.

Make certain all potential lenders read your business plan first. Then encourage them to ask questions. They may have useful suggestions about your business and funding, even if they don't invest.

Because raising outside money is difficult for fledgling businesses, the owners themselves are the number-one source of start-up capital, followed by friends and family. Owners typically use home equity loans, personal lines of credit, severance pay, and sometimes, with older people, lump sum retirement benefits. (See Chapter 5 on smart borrowing.) Be prepared to back up your idea with your own money. This doesn't mean committing your entire life savings, but be ready to toss in a substantial portion of start-up capital, often 50%. Doing so indicates your commitment to potential investors. If owners can't see the wisdom of investing in their own operation, why should anyone else? Beyond savings, additional sources of personal money might include: sale of an asset, such as a house, boat, land, stocks, or bonds; or a loan on a life insurance policy.

*Banks* and other institutional lenders are tough—usually they won't invest unless they have had a prior, successful dealing with the person. The challenge is to convince them to say yes even though they are predisposed to say no. The best weapons are an excellent business plan, commitment of personal capital, collateral (stocks, bonds, CDs, or other assets), and clear answers to these four questions:

1. Why do you need the money?
2. How much and for how long?

3. How will it be spent?

4. How and when will it be paid back?

Shop for banks by reading the ads in newspapers, asking other business owners where they got loans, and checking with accountants, lawyers, and insurance agents for referrals.

$$ ACTION TIP: Plan ahead. If at all possible, apply for a loan while still holding a job that provides regular paychecks. Once this steady stream of income is gone, most lenders turn down loan requests, citing lack of immediate income.

*Family and friends* are the most likely to invest with less expectation in return. Of course, when a business fails, friendships may be strained and family members may become alienated. Because money and emotions can be a dangerous mix, think matters through at the outset and approach only those people who can afford to lose their investment. Mail copies of the business plan with a personalized cover letter to each one. Friends, as well as total strangers are more likely to make a loan to the author of a solid business plan than to the person who casually calls with no warning, asking for money. Keep the arrangement businesslike, drawing up a loan agreement. To determine the interest rate, use the prime rate, the rate banks charge their top clients, or 1% over prime.

*The Small Business Administration* should be tapped if you can't get a bank loan. The SBA guarantees bank loans, up to $750,000, for qualified businesses. Borrowers can take up to twenty-five years to pay back the loan, although most pay them back in five to seven years. There is no prepayment penalty and rates fluctuate but are generally between 2¼% and 2¾% over prime. In addition, there's a flat loan guarantee fee of 2% of the total amount borrowed. Because the SBA guarantee on loans made by banks puts Uncle Sam on the line if borrowers don't pay up, loan applicants must have good credit as well as sufficient collateral. Under the Women's Business Ownership Act, the agency also administers a new federal program encouraging SBA-guaranteed loans of up to $50,000 to men or women. Be warned that applying for a loan is time-consuming. And, in return for guaranteeing your loan, the SBA will place restrictions on the business, controlling the amount of debt you can take on, for example.

$$ ACTION TIP: For information, call the SBA at 800-346-1614. For useful taped information on starting and financing a business, phone 800-368-5855.

## FIND A PARTNER

Many of the most successful small businesses began as a *partnership*—often one person with an idea, the other with cash, or two people, neither with quite enough cash. It worked for Ben and Jerry, Baskin and Robbins, Rolls and Royce, Johnson and Johnson. To eliminate problems, have a lawyer draw up a partnership agreement spelling out the amount invested by each partner, the procedures to use if additional cash is needed, the exact responsibilities of each, how the profits and losses will be divided, how each can leave the business, and how additional partners will be admitted.

## VENTURE CAPITALISTS

Another source of funding is venture capitalists, professional investors who help finance start-up companies they believe will go public or be bought out by large companies within a few years. In return, most want part control of the business, so proceed with caution.

$$ ACTION TIP: To find venture capitalists, check the

library for *Pratt's Guide to Venture Capital Sources*, published by Venture Economics. For current lists of venture capitalists, send a business-size, self-addressed stamped envelope and $7.50 to the National Association of Small Business Investment Companies, 1156 15th Street, NW, Suite 1101, Washington, DC 20005; 202-833-8230, and a 9 x 12 envelope with $1.85 in postage to the National Venture Capital Association, 1655 North Fort Myer Drive, Suite 700, Arlington, VA 22209, (703-528-4370).

Another option is to tap into a venture capital club which brings together entrepreneurs and investors. Call your local chamber of commerce for clubs in your area, or consult the *Directory of Venture Capital Clubs*, available at libraries or for $9.95 from the International Venture Capital Institute, Inc., P.O. Box 1333, Stamford, CT 06904 (203-323-3143).

$$ ACTION TIP: The IRS publishes a number of booklets that help business owners. For free copies, call 800-TAX-FORM.

#334 Tax Guide for Small Business

#587 Business Use of Your Home

#533 Self-Employment Tax

#463 Travel, Entertainment & Gift Expenses

#541 Tax Information on Partnership Income and Losses

## HELP FROM YOUR STATE

A 1990 survey by the National Conference of State Legislatures found that thirty-five states have programs to provide small business assistance in distressed areas, and legislation was pending in five other states. Of these, twenty-nine states have enacted measures to give tax incentives to businesses that locate or expand in distressed areas. Washington, for example, gives a $1,000 tax credit for each job created in an eligible business project. Programs to assist minority businesses have passed in twenty-eight states and fourteen states have programs to help female-owned businesses. Eastern states showed the biggest gains in female-owned firms.

# 5

# Credit, Debt, and the Cash Crunch

At some point in their lives, most people have experienced the consequences of too much debt or faced a cash shortage that threatens to undermine their financial well-being. Any large expense, like purchasing a home or paying college tuition, usually has to be financed; only the lucky few have the available funds to meet these events. Sometimes, particularly during a recession, the $3,000 needed to buy a used car is a hardship, or paying a $500 medical bill means some other debt will have to go unpaid. At these times, smart borrowing becomes one of your most valuable financial tools.

## IF YOU SEE A CASH CRUNCH COMING

Cash crunches can stem from positive events, such as the arrival of a new baby or voluntarily changing careers, or they can be the result of traumatic situations, such as being laid off or incurring significant medical bills. Cash crunches can happen to anyone, even the most affluent, tipping them into a financial tailspin.

If you face a financial crisis, you will certainly need a

quick fix, or maybe several of them, to tide you over. How dramatically you need to change your life-style depends on the extent of your shortfall. Coming up with $500 for a medical bill is not as painful as meeting college tuition payments. And knowing about the event in advance can make a difference in your ability to cope. If you have forewarning, try to adjust your life-style right away. But if an emergency comes out of the blue, be realistic and follow these steps immediately:

1. Evaluate your overall spending pattern.
2. Create a crisis budget (see pages 22–26).
3. Change your spending habits.
4. Don't wait for your creditors to hound you. Call and write to explain your problems. Most will accept partial payment.
5. Keep crucial bills paid—rent, utilities, mortgage, car, health and automobile insurance.
6. Refinance or renegotiate your loans.
7. Stop charging.
8. List all the assets you can liquidate—jewelry, an extra car, stocks, bonds, savings accounts, CDs, etc.

Most importantly, don't panic. There are many solutions and options to pursue:

*Don't sell assets in a panic*. Unloading one or two items, such as jewelry you don't wear or an extra car, is only a one-shot solution and might not be enough to solve your problem, especially if you're selling into a weak market. But if you hardly ever use the sailboat, then sell it. Better still, prioritize your assets and sell depreciated securities first. Up to $3,000 in losses each year can be used to offset income of any kind.

*Stop buying nonessentials*. Your first reflex when your income drops may be to reach for your credit card to maintain the life-style you're accustomed to. Don't. Your first priority is to pay the mortgage, medical, auto, and homeowners insurance premiums. In a crisis, put off funding your retirement plans, including your 401(k) in order to keep cash flow high.

*Tap the college account.* Stop putting money away for college tuition and if you need to, raid the account. This does not make you a terrible parent. But do explain it to your children if they are old enough to understand. If college is a long way off, you can refund the account later on. On the other hand, if it's just a few years away, a drop in income and savings could help your child qualify for financial aid. (See pages 140–144.)

*Don't sell the house.* This should always be your last resort. Borrow against it instead. But if paying the mortgage is a problem, call your lender right away and explain your circumstances. There will be more on mortgage refinancing later in this chapter.

If you still have a shortfall, consider a loan, but make sure you are a smart borrower.

## SMART WAYS TO BORROW

In order to get through the leaner days of the recession, you may need to borrow money. Whether you're in the market for a small loan or a major mortgage, you'll find that banks, savings and loan associations, credit unions, stockbrokers, automobile dealers, pawnshops, and loan sharks all sell cash—for a price known as interest. When selecting a lender, factor in not only interest rates and fees but also the current tax rules, since not all types of interest are tax-deductible.

Before taking out a loan, ask yourself:

1. Do I really need to borrow?
2. Can I use savings?

3. Can I sell stocks, bonds, a second car, or other asset(s)?
4. Can I take a second job or free-lance to make money?

If you can answer yes to questions two through four, we advise you to first try these alternatives. Too much debt and living on credit is what got us here in the first place. If you do need a loan, get the best deal possible. Look at the chart on pages 124–125 and draw up a list of questions to ask lenders. Remember, the shorter the duration of the loan, the lower the total interest, but the higher the monthly payments.

To borrow wisely:

1. *Stop in at your local bank first*. You may get a lower rate or faster approval if you're an established customer with an account.

2. *Check your credit union*. These nonprofit institutions have low overhead and often provide more favorable loan rates to members than banks and S&Ls. To find out if you can join a credit union, call the Credit Union National Association at 608-231-4044.

3. *Comparison shop*. Rates and terms vary at all institutions, even among banks in the same town.

4. *Try for a secured loan first*. If you can put up collateral (stocks, bonds, real estate, etc.), interest rates will be lower than on unsecured loans which are based on your signature.

5. *Monitor interest rates*. Many loans are adjustable, moving up and down with the prime rate or other key rate, such as the rate paid on Treasury bills. If you get an adjustable loan, make certain you can handle any increase should rates move up. A 1% increase on a $100,000, thirty-year loan will boost your monthly payment by $78 and wind up costing $28,080 more in total. And be sure to get a cap—the top interest rate you can be charged.

6. *Negotiate the interest rate*. Most people accept the stated rate. But try to negotiate. One or two percentage points makes a big difference over time. For example, a one-percentage-point reduction on a $100,000, thirty-year home mortgage can save you $27,000; a reduction of a half a point, $13,500.

7. *Ditto on fees*. A good credit rating and a long-term relationship with the bank may enable you to knock down some fees.

8. *Show up prepared*. If you are informed, the bank will regard you as a good businessperson. For example, if you apply for a car loan, know the model of car you will be buying, the amount you plan to put down, and precisely how long you need the loan for. If you don't know what papers you'll need to bring, call and ask ahead of time. For certain loans you need tax returns, a business plan, etc.

9. *Don't give up after being turned down*. Your application may be accepted by some banks and turned down by others. If it is turned down, ask to speak with the loan officer's boss. If it's turned down at that level, ask why. Then move on to another bank.

## LOAN LINGO

Understand these terms before borrowing a penny:

• *Adjustable rate loan:* A loan in which changes in the interest rate depend upon a key rate such as the prime rate or the rate paid on Treasury bills, as opposed to a fixed rate loan in which the rate remains the same throughout the loan period. The rate is adjusted periodically—every six or twelve months.

• *Annual percentage rate (APR):* The cost of credit expressed as an annual rate; it includes interest and any charges.

- *Assumability:* When a home is sold the seller may have the privilege of transferring the mortgage to the buyer. This makes it assumable. Usually the lender insists on some additional fee for allowing the mortgage to be assumed and will also insist on checking the credit standing of the buyer.
- *Balloon payment:* A final payment on a loan that is significantly larger than any preceding payments.
- *Buydown:* A home seller pays a certain amount to the lender so the lender will offer a lower rate for a certain period of time, to make it easier for the buyer to buy the home.
- *Cap:* A limit on how high an interest rate can go in an adjustable rate loan or mortgage.
- *Cash value:* The dollar amount a policyholder can borrow against a life insurance policy. This amount grows over time as dividends and premiums accumulate.
- *Conversion clause:* A section in an adjustable rate mortgage which allows you to convert your mortgage from an ARM to a fixed rate mortgage.
- *Equity:* The fair market value of a piece of property, minus the mortgaged amount left to be repaid; the amount of property you own outright.
- *Index:* The standard measure of changes in interest rates which is used by the lender to change the interest rates in an adjustable loan. Typical indices are the rates on Treasury bills or notes or the prime rate.
- *Interest:* Cost of borrowing money, stated as a percentage rate.
- *Margin account:* A brokerage account in which customers buy stocks and bonds with money borrowed from the broker. Cash loans are available, using the account as collateral.
- *Points:* Payments made to a lender to get a loan. One point equals one percentage point of the amount loaned. Points are usually tax-deductible.
- *Prime rate:* The rate charged to a bank's top-rated commercial clients. Used as a standard for other loans.
- *Principal:* The balance of a debt, excluding interest.
- *Vested:* The amount an employee has a right to receive from his or her retirement plan.

## Ways to Borrow Money

| Type of Loan | Where Available |
| --- | --- |
| • Check overdraft | Bank, S&L, credit union |
| • Secured loan | Bank, S&L, credit union |
| • Unsecured loan | Bank, S&L, credit union |
| • Credit card loan | Bank, S&L, credit union |
| • Home equity line | Bank, S&L, credit union |
| • Second mortgage | Bank, S&L, credit union |
| • Life insurance | Insurance company |
| • Margin loan | Stockbroker |
| • 401(k) | Your company |
| • Auto loan | Bank, S&L, credit union, car dealer |
| • Family and friends | Directly |
| • College tuition loan | Bank, federal government |

| *Rate | Best For | Disadvantages |
|---|---|---|
| 18% | Small purchases that can be covered quickly | High rates plus possible annual fee |
| 11.9 | Immediate cash; small amounts | Ties up collateral such as a CD |
| 17.4 | Emergency only | Very high rates |
| 18.8 | Emergency or major purchase | Avoid for small items; seductive |
| 11.2 | Large items: college tuition, remodeling, more property | Could lose home if borrower can't meet payments |
| 9.1 | Major items: real estate, etc. | Easy to overextend budget |
| 5–8 | Any purpose | May affect rest of policy |
| 12.2 | More stocks or bonds, or large items | Loan could be called if value of securities drop |
| 8.7 | Major reasons only | |
| 12.2 | Automobile | |
| (See page 130) | Important reasons | Can cause hard feelings |
| (See pages 141–143) | Education | Limited use |

*Rates as of January 14, 1991.

There are as many different places to shop for a loan as there are types of loans, rates, and terms. Before you borrow against your credit card or take out a second mortgage, consider these key points when applying for consumer, real estate, life insurance, or brokerage loans:

## CONSUMER LOANS

1. *Check overdrafts*. Many banks will cover checking account overdrafts. Because rates are high, use this only for small items or emergencies.

2. *Secured personal loans*. Banks will lend money using your savings account or CD as collateral. They charge 2–4% more than the rate they are paying on your deposit, the CD, or savings account you are using as collateral. If you have a "bundled" account, one that combines checking, savings, and stocks, for example, you may be able to borrow up to a certain percentage of the combined value of the account—sometimes at a slightly reduced rate. The chief advantage of bundled or combo accounts, however, is convenience and service; better deals may be available elsewhere. WARNING: If you fail to pay off a secured personal loan, the bank can deduct principal and interest payments from your deposit.

Self-disciplined people can skip a secured personal loan if a savings account is being used as collateral. Simply withdraw money from your savings account and pay it back as soon as possible. With a secured bank loan you are actually paying the bank to impose a repayment schedule, rather than doing it on your own. If you're using a CD as collateral, calculate the difference between the penalty for early withdrawal on your CD and the additional interest you will pay on the secured loan to determine your best course of action.

3. *Unsecured personal loans*. What if you don't have col-

lateral? You can still get a bank loan but you will have to pay 1–3% more than the rates on secured loans in your area. Unsecured lines of credit at banks, S&Ls, and credit unions give you access to cash in amounts from $2,000 to $25,000. The amount you qualify for depends on your income and credit rating. Most of these loans have a fixed rate of interest with three years to repay. WARNING: Late payment penalties and annual fees add to your costs.

$$ ACTION TIP: Some banks offer slightly lower rates if you maintain a sizable deposit ($10,000) in your checking account. The line of credit is then attached to this account.

4. *Credit card loans.* You can tap a line of credit on your Visa, MasterCard, or almost any other bank card by simply writing a check. Rates are *extremely high*. WARNING: Easy to arrange, these loans are seductive and should be used only in an emergency until you can negotiate a better deal elsewhere. There's one exception, however. With a Sears' Discover credit card you can borrow up to your credit limit for fifty days at an annual rate below 2%. The typical initial credit limit is $2,000, but you can apply for a higher limit by calling 800-DISCOVE. And you can get such loans six times a year. Discover also allows cardholders to get cash advances up to their credit limit *without owing interest* if they pay back the money within a twenty-five-day grace period. Discover has no annual fee in forty-eight states, and in North Carolina and Wisconsin it's $15. CAUTION: In order to avoid owing Discover's usual 19.8% financing charge, you must clear your account balance in full the month before and the month after the cash advance appears on your statement. There is a transaction fee equal to 2.5% of the cash advance, with a minimum charge of $2 and a maximum of $10.

5. *Secured credit cards.* A growing number of banks loan money on a Visa or MasterCard that has been "secured" by a deposit with the bank. Your credit line is based on the amount on deposit with the bank. The typical minimum is $500 to

$3,000. Use only a bank that pays interest on your deposit. WARNING: The bank can tap your deposit if your payments are late.

6. *Auto loans*. Banks, finance companies, and auto dealers offer installment-type auto loans for new and used cars. The lowest rates are generally offered by banks to customers who agree to have payments automatically deducted from their savings or checking account. Still, low-rate financing from dealers will be available as long as there's a slump in auto sales. The best financing deals are those with the shortest term because automakers figure that the sooner you pay off your car loan, the sooner you'll buy a new one. If the choice is between a low-rate loan and a rebate, you're probably better off taking the rebate and getting the financing from a bank or use a home equity loan—interest is deductible.

$$ ACTION TIP: If the dealer's rate is significantly lower than the bank's, the dealer may have raised the price on the car to subsidize the loan rate. Ask how much the car would cost if you paid cash and get it in writing.

## REAL ESTATE LOANS

1. *Home equity loans*. These "evergreen" loans give home owners a line of credit or the right to borrow up to a specified dollar amount determined by the lender. After getting the loan approval, you simply write a check whenever you need money. Repayment terms vary: Some lenders require payment of principal plus interest on a regular basis, while with others, you pay interest regularly and the principal is due in a balloon payment upon expiration of the loan. The length of the credit line may be fixed or open-ended, and most home equity loans have variable rates. The pros and cons of these loans are discussed in detail on page 133.

2. *Secondary mortgages*. These mortgages, which run from ten to twenty-five years, provide a lump sum of cash up

front. Borrowers then make regular monthly payments to the lender.

With both types of real estate loans, the amount available is determined by the equity you've built up in your home and your ability to repay the debt. Rates are relatively low because the lien against your property gives the lender protection in case you default on your payments. Ask about fees and closing costs, which can be hefty, before signing on the dotted line.

## LIFE INSURANCE LOANS

You can borrow against the cash value of universal and whole life policies for any purpose and repay the loan when you wish. On older policies, rates may be as low as 4–5%, while rates on newer policies run much higher depending on the type of insurance and the insured's age. WARNING: Some companies reduce the amount of interest they pay on the money left inside the policy when you take out a loan. And any outstanding amount left when you die will be deducted from the amount of money due to your beneficiaries.

## BROKERAGE LOANS

With a margin account at a brokerage firm, you can borrow up to 50% of the value of the assets your broker holds. If the loan is used to buy investments, interest is deductible up to the amount of investment income earned. The interest rate on a brokerage loan is one of the lowest you'll find—½ to 1½ points above the broker call rate, the rate banks charge brokerage firms. This type of loan is suitable only for sophisticated investors. WARNING: You must maintain 25 to 30% of equity in your account. If the value of your securities drops below this amount, you will receive a margin call from your broker asking you to meet the equity minimum with cash or additional collateral. If you are unable to do this, the broker has a right to sell your securities to bring the account up to the minimum requirement.

## BORROWING FROM FAMILY AND FRIENDS

*Neither a borrower nor a lender be*
*for loan oft loses both itself and friend . . .*
*Hamlet*, Act I, Scene 3

Keep Polonius' advice to Laertes in mind as you consider asking a close friend or relative for money. Borrowing from family or friends is in many ways the most painful loan and most people turn to it last, after other sources of credit have been exhausted. Yet there are some perfectly good reasons to put it first.

It's a good solution if you need cash only for a short term and you are certain that the lender can afford it and that you will pay it back. It is often less expensive than quick loans from banks or credit cards. And quite often friends and relatives, aware of your problems, may really welcome a chance to help you out and show their support. Older family members who are in the process of reducing their future estate tax may be willing to loan you some part of what, in the future, they were planning to give you as an inheritance.

If you decide to go this route, do so in a businesslike way. Get a standard loan note from your local stationery store, sign and date it, and give it to the lender. The note should include the date of loan, date when due, and interest rate. Set up due dates instead of "payment on demand" because this may become an embarrassment to the lender who must then call you to initiate repayment. You should assume responsibility for repayment dates.

$$ ACTION TIP: When seeking a loan from family members or friends, ask for a formal meeting by telephone or

write a letter to discuss the topic. This gives the potential lender a way to say no without embarrassing either of you. The worst time to request money is at a family dinner. If you do get the loan, insist on paying interest, even if it's below the going rate. Use prime, the rate banks charge their most creditworthy customers, as a guideline. It is listed on the financial pages of most large newspapers, in the *Wall Street Journal*, and *Barron's*.

## TAPPING YOUR PENSION PLAN OR RETIREMENT SAVINGS

If things get tough enough, you may have to turn to your company's pension plan or your own IRA to raise emergency cash. But between the IRS and your company, the rules are ridiculously complicated. Here are the basics, but be certain to discuss your moves with your company's pension or benefits officer and an accountant.

### WITHDRAWING MONEY

• *401(k) plans*. You may not withdraw funds from your 401(k) unless you are fifty-nine and one-half years old, lose your job, become disabled, or are able to show financial hardship. Financial hardship is defined by the IRS as an immediate and heavy financial need that cannot be met by other financial resources. It includes the purchase of a home; college expenses for you, your spouse, or child; medical expenses; funeral expenses for a member of your immediate family; or mortgage foreclosure. You will have to pay income tax on this money plus a 10% penalty for premature withdrawals.

• *IRAs*. If you take money out of your IRA before you are fifty-nine and a half, and you are not disabled, you will be hit with a 10% penalty on the amount you take out. In addition, you will have to pay income tax on the amount withdrawn.

Unlike a 401(k), however, IRAs impose no hardship conditions on withdrawals.

$$ ACTION TIP: You can withdraw money from each of your IRAs for sixty days, once a year, with no penalty. If the money is not repaid to your account within sixty days, you will have to pay income taxes on the amount outstanding plus a 10% penalty. If you have two IRAs, you can stagger borrowing dates and have access to your money for 120 days. WARNING: Use this only if you are certain you can pay the money back in time.

## BORROWING MONEY

• *IRAs*. Borrowing against an IRA should be avoided: The IRS regards this as taking out the entire amount even if you've taken only part of it, and your IRA loses its tax-deferred status. If you pledge any part of your IRA for a loan, the pledged part is considered a distribution—incurring a 10% penalty.

• *Retirement plans*. Most companies let employees borrow against the money they have in their retirement plans—up to 50% of the amount vested, or $50,000, whichever is less. Usually you must repay all the money in installments over a period no longer than five years through payroll deductions. However, loans to buy a primary residence can run longer. Finance charges are based on current market rates—you can expect to pay the prime rate plus one or two percentage points. Terms vary, so check with your benefits officer.

Obviously, you should tap your retirement funds with great care and only after you have exhausted all other means—sold your stocks and bonds, used your savings account, and sold luxury items.

## HOME EQUITY LOANS

If you have an outstanding loan on your automobile, a bank loan, and you continually run up a huge loan balance on your credit cards, you might want to consider consolidating these loans and taking out a home equity loan. You will get a significantly lower interest rate with a home equity loan and the interest you pay is tax-deductible. (Interest on other types of consumer loans is no longer tax-deductible.) Before you do, however, you should know the pitfalls of this type of credit.

A home equity loan is a form of revolving credit in which your house or apartment serves as collateral. Because your home is probably your most important asset, pledge it against a loan very carefully and only to consolidate more expensive loans or to pay for big-ticket items, such as college education, medical bills, or a necessary home improvement. Never put your home on the line for a new Jaguar with which to impress the neighbors or to help with day-to-day expenses.

With a home equity loan, the bank gives you a line of credit, based on a percentage of the appraised value of your home minus the mortgage. If it's a 75% loan and your home is worth $200,000, and you have a $90,000 mortgage, you would be offered a home equity loan of $60,000. (Seventy-five percent of your home's value, $150,000, minus the $90,000 mortgage equals $60,000.) Bankers provide home equity cash in one of two ways. A *closed-end loan* gives you the cash in a lump sum and you repay it according to a fixed schedule, usually over fifteen or twenty years. The interest rate may be set or adjustable. One kind of adjustable plan includes a balloon feature: The loan balance is due in full every three years and is refinanced at the current rate. WARN-ING: If you turn out to be a poor credit risk, the bank can deny you refinancing.

The second type of loan extends you *a line of credit*. Once you receive approval, you may borrow any amount up to the limit anytime you wish. You tap the money with special checks, a credit card, or vouchers provided by the bank. Typically the first cash advance has a $1,000 minimum. Thereafter you can borrow in increments of, say, $500 or $1,000.

Most line-of-credit loans are adjustable. There will be a minimum monthly payment.

**$$ ACTION TIP:** Be wary of lenders who encourage you to tie up your equity. If you get an open-end line of credit for $20,000, and you use only $10,000, you've really locked up $20,000. Other lenders will consider you in debt for the total amount, not just the portion you've used. You may not be able to borrow elsewhere until you clean up your line of credit.

**$$ ACTION TIP:** Don't be dazzled by the lower interest rate and tax break on this loan. Unless you are disciplined, you could fall into the trap of easy credit and go into too much debt. With home prices tumbling, many earlier borrowers find that their home equity is substantially reduced and their two mortgages—first mortgage and home equity loan—leaves them critically exposed.

*What to look for:* Be sure you know all the costs involved for setting up a home equity loan. There are many. Find out what the interest rate is and, if it's adjustable, what the index is. How frequently will the rate change? Is there a cap? Can the loan be converted to a fixed rate loan?

---

## COSTS OF A HOME EQUITY LOAN

- An appraisal fee to determine the value of your house.
- An application fee.
- Points—one point equals one percent of the total credit limit.
- Closing costs.
- Annual maintenance fee.
- Transaction fees.

---

Many lenders allow you to pay *interest only* on your loan, with a balloon payment of the full amount due at the end of the term. This is just like offering pie and ice cream to someone on a strict diet. You must ask yourself: Can I handle the open-ended temptation of a line of credit?

## FINANCING YOUR HOME

For most of us, our home is our most valuable asset and our mortgage payment our largest monthly bill. In a recession, both of these facts take on added importance. The value of your home becomes a critical part of your net worth, yet with the collapse of real estate prices in many parts of the country, Americans have had to recalculate their net worth in sharply lower terms. Moreover, the burden of meeting monthly mortgage payments becomes heavier when incomes drop, jobs are lost, or working hours reduced.

Banks throughout the country have suffered and continue to suffer loan losses and loan postponements because of the poor real estate market. And the collapse of large savings and loan companies hasn't helped. Many of the country's largest insurance companies, who are the traditional providers of long-term mortgage money for commercial real estate, have been heavily involved and the full damage to many of these institutions is still not known. The nation's most respected names in banking and insurance are heavily involved in real estate loans of dubious value. Where does this leave you? And what can you do to cope during the recession? First, let's look at the two different types of mortgages.

## ADJUSTABLE RATE MORTGAGES

Called ARMs for short, these generally offer lower *initial* rates than fixed-rate mortgages. However, the rate and the monthly payment move up and down, based on an index tied to an interest rate figure, such as the rate on Treasury bills or notes. The lower initial rate makes ARMs attractive to people who expect their income to rise enough to cover the potential increases in monthly payments if rates rise. They are also appealing to those who don't expect to remain in their home more than a few years.

Yet ARMs are risky. Interest rates could rise significantly after you take on an ARM. For an ARM to be worth this risk, the initial rate should be at least two percentage points lower than the fixed rate. Still, you may not want to assume that risk with your home.

The interest rate on an ARM is typically adjusted every six months, annually, or once every three years. Some ARMS are convertible into fixed-rate loans during a certain time period, usually between the second and fifth year. You should ask for this protection when taking out an ARM.

## FIXED-RATE MORTGAGES

These old-fashioned mortgages are generally best for those who plan to remain in their homes for some time. With a fixed-rate mortgage, you know what your payments will be, which makes budgeting a lot easier than with an ARM. And for most people, as time passes the mortgage payment becomes a smaller and smaller portion of their income and is therefore easier and easier to handle. But there is a price for this certainty and that is a higher monthly payment at the beginning than with an ARM. Bankers generally require that housing expenses, including real estate taxes and monthly maintenance payments on a cooperative apartment or condominium, are not more than 28% of your gross income.

If you have sufficient income, the fifteen-year mortgage allows you to pay for your home in fifteen years. Of course, monthly payments are higher. This type of mortgage is good for those nearing retirement—you certainly don't want to be strapped with mortgage payments when you stop working.

Yet another variation on the theme is biweekly payments, which allows you to pay off the mortgage even faster.

## LEASE-OPTION AGREEMENTS

If you own a house you'd like to sell but haven't been able to, or if you want to buy but can't quite afford the downpayment or secure a mortgage, the lease-option plan may solve your problem. With the lease option, the potential buyer moves into the house as a tenant, paying rent each month. The rent, however, is much higher than normal, often double. For example, if the rent would be $600, under the lease-option plan the person might pay $1,200. The extra amount is credited toward the down payment. Sometimes there's an up-front cash payment as well, anywhere from $1,000 to $5,000 or more. Then, at the end of a specified time period, typically one to five years, the tenant finds a mortgage and buys the house. WARNING: If he or she still can't afford it, the owner keeps all the extra payments.

Most of these arrangements come about through ads in local newspapers, since real estate brokers seldom handle them because of low commissions and the long waiting period until the sale goes through.

## DOES IT PAY TO REFINANCE?

If you have an old high-rate mortgage, refinancing might make sense. The rule of thumb is that a new mortgage must be at least two percentage points lower than the existing one to make up for the heavy up-front fees charged by bankers. These fees can run 3–4% of the total loan. In addition, you must take into consideration how long you will be staying in your house. Plan on three years minimum to recoup the expenses of refinancing. In other words, the biggest cost of refinancing is the bank's up-front fee or points. And the sooner you plan to move, the greater the rate differential must be between your old and your new mortgages for refinancing to make sense.

$$ ACTION TIP: With interest rates heading down in the

recession, it usually makes sense to refinance, provided you meet the criteria described above.

## MORTGAGE PROBLEMS

If you are having difficulties meeting your mortgage payments, something that happens to thousands of Americans during economic slowdowns, there are steps you can take to resolve the situation. Home owners will find, for the most part, that bankers will be quite willing to work with them. Banks do not want to foreclose—it's an expensive process and during that time they don't receive any payments. Most property needs repairs before it can be sold, and the bottom line is that lenders take a loss of 40–50% of the original mortgage.

Instead, lenders will discuss reworking your loan. This can mean a number of things. Not that you will owe less, but the bank will allow you to make smaller payments for several months and catch up later. The key factor in this situation is for you to call the lender, explain your situation, and ask for an appointment to try to resolve it. Bankers look favorably upon borrowers who take the initiative and don't hide their cash shortfall. You will be asked to show your banker your business and individual income tax returns, your assets, including your retirement plans, life insurance, stocks, bonds, child-support payments, etc.; as well as your liabilities, including car payments, credit card debt, and medical bills. The loan officer will work with you and possibly your other creditors to find a solution.

### Foreclosure

People in a really desperate financial condition often think about abandoning their mortgage. But foreclosure has several serious and long-term repercussions. First, it stays on your credit record for seven years and can make it difficult to get new credit of any kind. Banks regard the manner in which people handle their mortgage as the number-one indicator of their overall creditworthiness. Foreclosure can, in some cases, mean losing existing credit cards. And if it's a soft real estate market, the house may not bring in enough at a foreclosure auction to cover the remaining mortgage. Consequently, more and more lenders are forcing the home owner/borrower to make up the difference. They can do this by repossessing your car or garnishing paychecks, a process known as "deficiency judgments."

If you are financially strapped and unable to work out a solution with your banker, you might be better off to file for personal bankruptcy (see page 145), although this should absolutely be your very last option. In some states, but not all, the owner is allowed to keep his or her house, even if it isn't paid for, because this type of property does not fall into the bankruptcy estate. CAUTION: Bankruptcy stays on your credit record for ten years.

## FINANCING A COLLEGE EDUCATION

Aside from buying a home, your child's college tuition will probably be one of your family's biggest expenses. Education is an investment you can't afford not to make. Fortunately, there are ways you can plan ahead and get financial aid when the day comes that your child is college-bound.

$$ ACTION TIP: For a comprehensive look at financing college tuition, send $4.50 to *Money* magazine, "*Money* Guide to College," P.O. Box 30626, Tampa, FL 33630-0626, for their special issue, "*Money* Guide to America's Best College Buys (1990)."

Economizing is essential. The annual cost of a four-year private college now averages $12,635 and is increasing between 6–8% a year. State universities for in-state students are considerably less expensive but still not cheap: Annual costs average $6,594. Community colleges are just under $900. Yet there are many top-rated colleges and universities that are relatively reasonable. Two magazines, *U.S. News & World Report* and *Money*, list them every year. You will discover that one year of tuition at Harvard or Yale buys two years at the University of California at Los Angeles; Swarthmore and Amherst cost about one-third more than Washington and Lee University. Be open to these less expensive options. Other ways to save: have your student commute to college or participate in a work-study program.

$$ ACTION TIP: There is no gift tax on any amount paid toward a child's educational expenses provided the money goes directly to the institution. This works for grandparents as well.

## GETTING FINANCIAL AID

During the recession, more students will be applying for fewer available loans. If you think there's any possibility that you could qualify for some aid, it's worth going through the application process. No matter how many schools your child applies to, you probably need to complete only one of two forms: the College Scholarship Service's Financial Aid Form or the American College Testing's Family Financial Statement. Both are available from your high school guidance office, usually in November. The CSS or ACT determines your need for financial aid and sends this analysis to the colleges you select.

Before you apply, however, it pays to arrange your family's finances in a way that will increase the possibility you'll qualify for aid. Here's how:

1. *Pay off consumer loans* by taking out a home equity loan. Unlike auto and credit card debt, home equity loans are counted against assets on both the Financial Aid Form and the Family Financial Statement.

2. *Reduce your child's assets*. You're better off with assets in your name, not your child's. A full 35% of a student's

assets are expected to go toward college expenses, while parents are expected to contribute only between 5–6% of theirs.

$$ ACTION TIP: The Uniform Gifts to Minors Act does not allow you to transfer funds from your child's account to yours, but if your child is in need of a computer, or even a car for college, consider buying it out of his or her savings while in high school. And use your child's savings to pay the first year's tuition—this will help increase the amount of financial aid you might receive in the subsequent years of college.

3. *Give a conservative estimate* when evaluating your home. The recession is a plus in this case because home values are down in many areas of the country, yet your last tax assessment may overstate the value.

## Federal Aid

Part of the Financial Aid Form is for federal aid—the Pell Grant, Stafford loan, PLUS loan, and others. You must apply for federal aid to be eligible for other grants, loans, and work-study programs from the colleges. And you might get some help:

- *Stafford Loan*. If the cost of college is more than your assessed family contribution, freshmen and sophomores can borrow up to $2,625 a year and juniors and seniors up to $4,000. Interest rate: 8% for the first four years; 10% afterwards.

- *PLUS* (Parent Loans to Undergraduate Students). Regardless of financial need, the government loans parents up to $4,000 a year for an undergraduate. Interest rate: 3.75% above the fifty-two week Treasury bill rate, with a 12% cap.

- *SLS* (Supplemental Loan to Students). Independent students (those not living at home or receiving any financial support from parents) may borrow up to $4,000 a year. Interest rate: same as for PLUS.

## Other Methods to Finance Tuition

There are many avenues to explore in financing your child's education. You should:

1. *Ask the financial aid officer lots of questions*. Can you avoid tuition increases by paying for four years at the outset? Can tuition be paid in installments over ten months?

2. *Inquire about other aid sources*. Your employer may offer interest-free loans or special scholarships. You may be able to borrow from your profit-sharing or 401(k) plan. Check out local churches and synagogues, fraternal orders, police departments, and other local organizations. Many have special scholarships for local children.

$$ ACTION TIP: One of the most useful books on this topic is *Don't Miss Out: The Ambitious Student's Guide to Financial Aid*, available for $6.95 from Octamerson Associates, Box 2748, Alexandria, VA 22301.

3. *Look into a home equity loan*. It allows you to borrow up to 75% of the appraised value of your house minus the outstanding mortgage. (See page 133.)

4. *Look into commercial loans*. Many commercial loans have lower interest rates than the government's PLUS loans. But stay away from loans that have a nonrefundable application fee or a prepayment penalty.

## COMMERCIAL LOANS FOR COLLEGE STUDENTS

- *TERI*. The Education Resource Institute, 330 Stuart Street, Boston, MA 02116; 800-255-8374, provides loans of up to $20,000 annually with twenty years to prepay. Interest rate: prime plus 1 or 2%.

- *NELLIE MAE*. The New England Marketing Corp., 50 Braintree Hill Park, Suite 300, Braintree, MA 02184; 800-634-9308, offers loans called EXCEL and SHARE which can be secured by a home equity loan. Interest rate: prime plus 2 to 4%.

- *SALLIE MAE*. The Student Loan Marketing Association, 1050 Thomas Jefferson Street, NW, Washington, DC 20007; 800-292-6868 or 202-333-8000, has a wide range of grad and undergrad loans. Some let you borrow up to $10,000 a year or more if tuition is higher. Interest rate: Treasury bill rate plus several points.

- *PLATO*. University Support Services, 205 Van Buren Street, Suite 200, Herndon, VA 22070; 800-767-5626, lets you borrow up to $25,000 with fifteen years to repay. Interest rate: 3.85% above commercial paper.

$$ ACTION TIP: Take a new look at EE savings bonds. These pay a floor of 6% if held for at least five years. After that, the rate is adjusted every six months, based on the average rate paid on five-year Treasury notes. The rate as of January 1, 1991, was 7.01%. Although interest earned on these bonds has always been exempt from state and local taxes, the interest earned on bonds purchased after January 1, 1991, that are used to pay college tuition is also exempt from federal taxes. Parents' total income must fall below a certain dollar amount at the time the bonds are cashed in. The cap is adjusted annually for inflation. The tax break begins to phase out on incomes above $60,000 for couples and $40,000 for

singles and disappears altogether at $90,000 for couples and $55,000 for singles. Bonds purchased under this "tax-free education plan" cannot be held in the child's name. For full details, send 50 cents to the Consumer Information Center, Dept. 444X, Pueblo, CO 81009, for the pamphlet "U.S. Savings Bonds: Now Tax-Free for Education."

## CREDIT AS A WAY OF LIFE

Americans love to spend, and for many that means falling into debt. It's almost a national characteristic and it begins quite early in life, typically when parents let their children use credit cards for emergencies while away from home. A few years later, as seniors in college, they are bombarded with credit card applications. And it never ends. And when there's a recession, many who thought they were in good financial shape find they are drowning in debt. *You can stay out of trouble* if you:

- Keep your consumer credit payments to *no more* than 20% of your take-home pay. This does not include your mortgage. Housing expenses including mortgage should be under 35%.
- Don't let your credit card company increase your limit just because you're a good customer. Live within the old limit.
- Pay your credit card balance in full every month.
- Don't use a cash advance from one card to make a payment on another. You'll just end up with more bills to pay.

$$ ACTION TIP: Keep your credit record spanking clean. Once a year, find out what's in your credit file. Bankcard Holders of America, a consumer advocacy group, will send you a directory of all credit bureaus in your area so you can locate your file. The booklet contains instructions for investigating and repairing any credit errors. Send $2 to B.H.A.,

Credit Check Kit, 560 Herndon Parkway, Suite 120, Herndon, VA 22070. The same group tallies fifty banks across the country that offer low credit card interest rates. Send $1.50 and ask for the "Fair Deal Banks" list.

## REBUILDING YOUR CREDIT

If you've had trouble with credit, or have never established a borrowing history, you can get credit by obtaining a secured credit card. This is a Visa or MasterCard issued by a bank in exchange for depositing money (several hundred to a thousand dollars) at the bank. Your credit limit will be low and the deposit is frozen for as long as you have the card but if you use the card and make regular, on-time payments you will have built a good credit history. Bankcard Holders of America (see above for address) offers a "Secured Card" list for $3.

## BANKRUPTCY: LOOK BEFORE YOU LEAP

The billionaire brothers Nelson and Herbert Hunt did it. Former Texas governor John Connally did it. But you should think twice about declaring personal bankruptcy. No matter what you hear about it being easy or the latest trend, bankruptcy is a major financial decision which has serious, long-lasting implications. It is not an easy way out of debt. It is truly a last resort. Before declaring bankruptcy, if you're bogged down under a pile of bills and collection notices, get to a nonprofit credit counselor. (See page 147.)

First of all, bankruptcy stays on your credit record for ten years and can make it virtually impossible to get credit during that period. It raises a red flag every time you want to buy a car or home. (To get any type of mortgage, car loan, or personal line of credit, you will need a 30% deposit and/or a creditworthy cosigner, both of which may be difficult to come up with.) Your major credit cards are taken away and without even one, it's extremely difficult to rent a car or even write a check in most places. (To get a new credit card you will have to go for a secured card which involves depositing a considerable sum of money in escrow with the bank.) Renting an apartment or getting a job may be a problem, especially if your record makes landlords and employers nervous. That's not the end of it. If you owe the IRS, you still have to pay up. Child-support payments must be made, your IRA assets liquidated, and you'll be slapped with income tax on the earnings and a 10% early withdrawal penalty.

There are two types of personal bankruptcy. In declaring Chapter 7 bankruptcy, you surrender most of your property to be liquidated and the proceeds are then distributed to creditors. Chapter 7 lets you shelter limited, specified property, such as some personal items and some equity in your home, but most assets must be turned over to the court-appointed trustee. In Chapter 13, you present to a judge a financial plan that shows an honest attempt to repay most of your debts from future income.

Although there are justifiable times for bankruptcy and sometimes it's the only way out of really deep trouble, try credit counseling first.

$$ ACTION TIP: For a free pamphlet entitled "What You Should Know Before Declaring Bankruptcy," send a self-addressed stamped envelope to the American Financial Services Association, 1101 14th Street, NW, Washington, DC 20005.


## CREDIT COUNSELING

If creditors are hounding you or if you've been thinking about declaring bankruptcy, it's time for credit counseling. This step will help restore your dignity and your credit rating. About 35% of the people who go for counseling can avoid bankruptcy, according to the National Foundation for Consumer Credit, a nonprofit group in Silver Spring, Maryland, which represents 500 Consumer Credit Counseling Centers.

Credit counselors put a family on a repayment program and intervene with creditors to negotiate extended terms. You wind up having to make only one payment per month. The typical fee for this service, which is confidential, is $10 to $12 a month. When you go, they will ask for information about your income and debts. You will find making up this list is helpful in getting on the road to solvency. They will also ask you to give up your credit cards and take up a pay-as-you-go-with-cash policy.

$$ ACTION TIP: Call the National Foundation for Consumer Credit, 800-388-2227, and ask for the closest Consumer Credit Counseling office. Do not go to an expensive, for-profit agency; these so-called "credit clinics" charge exorbitant fees, and many use unscrupulous means to get at and repair negative information in your credit file.

Living on credit need not be a way of life; using the best resources available to get out of debt should be. By following the borrowing techniques included in this chapter, you should be able to achieve the financial security you deserve.

# 6

# The Energy Crunch

ENERGY conservation and the rising cost of gasoline at the pumps is on everybody's mind these days. As 1990 came to a close, concern for the environment and the possibility of a disruption to the world oil supply because of the conflict in the Persian Gulf were foremost in everyone's minds. But energy—heating your home, filling your gas tank—is also expensive. Cutting energy consumption cuts costs. But energy is something we all need and use—no matter how costly—and you can continue to prosper in the recession by investing in the right energy stocks. (See page 159.)

## HOW TO BECOME AN ENERGY MISER

Energy conservation is back in vogue, even though our costs are just about the lowest in the world. (In Europe, for example, the price of gasoline hovers around $5.00 per gallon.) Yet with the recent events in the Persian Gulf, the cost of energy is expected to rise to painful levels. And higher fuel costs, along with a recession, is a double whammy on the pocketbook. Turning off the lights and television set will help, but there's a great deal more you can do. For each degree you lower your thermostat in the winter, your fuel costs are cut by about 3%. In fact, lowering it by six degrees will save two barrels of oil and that in turn means that a little over 1,800 pounds of carbon monoxide will *not* be added to our atmosphere. So look for as many ways as possible to really slash energy costs and consumption. Begin with home heating and water heating costs — these two energy gobblers add up to about 75% of the energy you use.

$$ ACTION TIP: Get the whole family together and point out the importance of energy saving, money saving, and the recession. Efficient energy conservation is not only a way to save money; it's environmentally sound. Everyone benefits from being a cooperative good citizen of Earth.

---

### Con Edison
## Energy Conservation Checklist

| Kitchen | Yes | No |
|---|---|---|

**1. Refrigerator/freezer**

A. Refrigerator compartment

| | Yes | No |
|---|---|---|
| (a) Is the gasket undamaged and does it fit tightly around the door? | ☐ | ☐ |
| (b) Is there space between food items so air can circulate for cooling? | ☐ | ☐ |
| (c) Is the correct temperature setting being used for cooling? | ☐ | ☐ |
| (d) Are the condenser coils dust-free? | ☐ | ☐ |
| (e) If the refrigerator has a power-saver switch, do you use it to save electricity when the humidity is low? | ☐ | ☐ |
| (f) Do you think about what you need before opening the door? | ☐ | ☐ |

B. Freezer compartment

| | Yes | No |
|---|---|---|
| (a) Is the freezer packed with food? | ☐ | ☐ |
| (b) Is there less than ¼" buildup of ice? | ☐ | ☐ |
| (c) Is the correct temperature setting being used for freezing? | ☐ | ☐ |

---

**2. Range**

| | Yes | No |
|---|---|---|
| (a) Do you turn off the oven or surface units just before cooking is finished? | ☐ | ☐ |
| (b) Do you avoid preheating the oven unless it is necessary? | ☐ | ☐ |
| (c) Do you avoid opening the oven door while the food is cooking? | ☐ | ☐ |
| (d) Do you cook as many dishes in the oven at one time as you can instead of cooking each separately? | ☐ | ☐ |

# Energy Conservation Checklist

| 2. Range | Yes | No |
|---|---|---|
| (e) Do you use the lowest possible heat setting to cook foods on top of the range? | ☐ | ☐ |
| (f) Do you match the pot or pan to the size of the surface unit? | ☐ | ☐ |
| (g) Do you use tight-fitting covers on pots and pans when cooking? | ☐ | ☐ |

| 3. Dishwasher | | |
|---|---|---|
| (a) Is the dishwasher operated only with full loads? | ☐ | ☐ |
| (b) Do you stop the machine before the electric dry cycle and let the dishes air dry? | ☐ | ☐ |
| (c) Do you use the power-saver switch if the machine has one? | ☐ | ☐ |

| 4. Lighting | | |
|---|---|---|
| (a) Do you use fluorescent lighting where practical? | ☐ | ☐ |

| Bedroom | Yes | No |
|---|---|---|
| **Lighting** | | |
| (a) Do you use energy-saving bulbs for general lighting? | ☐ | ☐ |
| (b) Are the lights turned off when no one is in the room? | ☐ | ☐ |

| Bathroom | Yes | No |
|---|---|---|
| **Lighting** | | |
| (a) Are the lights turned off when not needed? | ☐ | ☐ |
| (b) Do you use fluorescent lighting where practical? | ☐ | ☐ |

| Living room | Yes | No |
|---|---|---|
| **Lighting** | | |
| (a) Do you use three-way bulbs where possible? | ☐ | ☐ |
| (b) Do you turn off lights when not needed? | ☐ | ☐ |
| (c) Are you using only the amount of light needed to do the job? | ☐ | ☐ |
| (d) Do you use energy-saving bulbs for general lighting? | ☐ | ☐ |

## Con Edison
# Energy Conservation Checklist

| Heating | Yes | No |
|---|:---:|:---:|
| (a) If you can control your own thermostat, do you set it no higher than 68 degrees during the day and 60 degrees at night? | ☐ | ☐ |
| (b) If a room is too warm and you can control the radiator, do you turn the radiator down or off instead of opening the window? | ☐ | ☐ |
| (c) Are the radiators dust-free? | ☐ | ☐ |
| (d) Do you close the drapes or blinds at night to keep in the heat? | ☐ | ☐ |
| (e) Do you open the drapes or blinds on sunny winter days to let in the heat of the sun? | ☐ | ☐ |
| (f) Are the radiators unblocked? | ☐ | ☐ |
| (g) Do you use interior plastic storm windows to prevent heat loss? | ☐ | ☐ |
| (h) Have you installed weatherstripping around windows and doors to reduce drafts? | ☐ | ☐ |
| (i) Have you notified your landlord or superintendent if there is steam or water coming out of the radiator vent? | ☐ | ☐ |

| Air conditioning | Yes | No |
|---|:---:|:---:|
| (a) Is the filter clean? | ☐ | ☐ |
| (b) Is the temperature control set so that the room is no cooler than 78°? | ☐ | ☐ |
| (c) Is the air conditioner turned off when you're away from the apartment? | ☐ | ☐ |
| (d) Do you use a timer for your air conditioner? (If the answer is "Yes," then answer question (e).) | ☐ | ☐ |
| (e) Is the timer set to turn the unit on no more than ½ hour before you expect to get home? | ☐ | ☐ |
| (f) Are the drapes or blinds closed during the day in summer? | ☐ | ☐ |
| (g) Do you use only a window fan when the outdoor temperature can provide cooling? | ☐ | ☐ |

| Miscellaneous | Yes | No |
|---|:---:|:---:|
| (a) Is the TV set or radio turned off when no one is in the room? | ☐ | ☐ |
| (b) Do you use modern, solid-state dimmer controls for lighting where practical? | ☐ | ☐ |
| (c) Do you use lower wattage lights in hallways and closets? | ☐ | ☐ |
| (d) Do you use automatic timers to turn lights on and off when needed? | ☐ | ☐ |

# KEEPING WARM

- Retrofitting a house with energy-efficient windows and doors, extra insulation, and weather stripping could cost several thousand dollars. Yet you'll reap a significantly lower utility bill as well as an almost dollar-for-dollar investment return if you sell your house.

- Although utility companies are no longer required by law to offer home energy audits to home owners, many still do—some for free, others for a fee. An inspector looks for airtightness, sufficient insulation, and overall energy efficiency. He or she will give a detailed list of suggestions for cutting consumption.

- A number of utility companies are switching to a "time-of-use" method of pricing for home owners. You pay more for electricity used during daytime peak hours than at night. If you're not home much during the day, you're almost certain to save by signing up for this program.

- If you heat with oil, an annual tune-up ($30–$90) can reduce oil consumption between 5% and 10%. Installing a flame-retention burner on an older system will further reduce consumption—perhaps by as much as 15%. These burners cost $450 to $600. They are standard equipment in oil-burning furnaces less than eight years old and on average consume 16% less fuel than older burners do.

- If you have forced-air heat, insulate the ducts that pass through unheated areas of the house. Clean the filter once a month.

- Regardless of the type of heat you have, check for leaks by moving a lighted candle around the frames of doors and windows. If it dances, you probably need caulking or weather stripping. Check holes where cable TV, antennas, and pipes enter the house.

- Invest in a programmable thermostat. You can automatically lower the heat at night (lopping off anywhere from 8–30% of your heating bills) and if no one's at home on weekdays, you can lower the heat then as well.

But that's not all. There are other steps everyone in the family can take to keep warm at lower costs.

- *Doors leak* every time they are opened. Don't stand around saying good-bye to friends with the front door open, and open it only as wide as needed.
- *Draft guards*—cloth tubes filled with sand—cover the cracks around windows and doors. These are a good solution for renters who don't want to assume the expense of new doors and storm windows.
- *Dress warmly*. Instead of racing for the thermostat when you wake up from a nap or come in from the cold, put on a sweater and warm socks. Europeans have been doing this for years!
- *Fireplace use*: Don't. It shoots heat up the chimney while heating up only the immediate area. Close the damper when not in use. Make certain it is tightly sealed, using fiber glass.
- *Move beds* away from cold areas such as windows.
- *Lower thermostats* when in bed and under the covers. Thermostats should not be located in a draft, giving incorrectly low readings.

## KEEPING LIGHT

It's not necessary to read by candlelight as Abe Lincoln had to do, but:

- Turn off the lights when they aren't needed and make sure everyone else does. (*It's not true* that switching lights on and off uses more energy than keeping them on.)
- Daylight is free. Use it as much as possible.
- Clean light bulbs for greater efficiency.

**153**

- Use light-colored lamp shades. Dark ones cut the light.
- Use low wattages when not reading or doing needlework.
- Fluorescent bulbs are more economical. Compact fluorescent bulbs cost about $10 but last ten times longer than the 95-cent conventional bulbs and use one-fourth the electricity. One of these fixtures can save about 300 pounds of coal from being burned. If they're not available at your hardware store, phone for the Seventh Generation catalog at 800-441-2538.
- Watch one television set at a time if you can do so without a war breaking out between family members. *Don't* use television as an electronic baby-sitter. *Teach your child to read.* (In this case, energy isn't wasted!)

## KEEPING CLEAN

The amount of energy used to heat water for washing everything from yourself to the dishes and clothes is second only to heating the house in terms of energy consumption. If the hot-water heater is warm when touched, wrap it in an insulation blanket. Also, insulate hot-water pipes where possible to reach. Next, install aerators in the faucets and flow restrictors in shower heads—these reduce hot water used for bathing by 50%. There are several other simple things to do:

- Turn off faucets all the way. One drop per second adds up to 700 gallons a year, and that's enough for fifty dishwasher loads.
- Full loads in the dishwasher, please. And, unless your dishwasher requires a higher temperature, lower it from 140 degrees to 120 degrees F. and save about 18% in heating energy.
- Full loads in the washing machine as well. And wash in cold water whenever possible. (See page 164). Set the rinse cycle for cold.

- When drying clothes get the lint out first, and don't over-dry them.
- Turn the iron off five minutes before you finish using it. It will still be hot, so the last five minutes are free. Also, consider drip-dry clothes!
- Showers? Keep them short. Hair dryers? Rub your hair dry with a towel first. A hair dryer uses as much energy as a toaster and if you have long hair you run it longer, too.

## KEEPING COOL

Americans spend more of their energy dollars on keeping cool than they do on keeping warm. Most brown-outs, which occur during peak load times, happen in the summer. So:

- Clean the air-conditioning filter at least once a month.
- Get a thermometer and keep your home at 78 degrees or higher. The costs escalate rapidly below 78: 75 degrees costs 18% more in energy and 72 degrees is 39% more.
- Don't leave the AC on when you're out. Buy a timer and set it to go on thirty minutes before you return.
- Open doors let in lots of warm air. It's the reverse of winter so be careful with unnecessary door action.
- Installing draft guards also saves money on air-conditioning.
- When you cook don't start a contest between the oven and the AC, with you paying money to two losing appliances. Shut off one or close the kitchen door.
- Get a window fan to bring in cool night air and take a load off your AC and your pocketbook.
- Pull down shades midday to keep out warm afternoon sunshine.

Many of the newer models of refrigerators are energy-efficient. Even with an older unit, you can cut costs by doing the following:

- Check the refrigerator and freezer condenser coils once a year. Clean off dirt and grime. If the refrigerator has a fan for circulating air, be sure the vent is clean and not obstructed.

- Cover liquids in the refrigerator. Added moisture makes the compressor work harder.

- Every time the door opens, the unit loses cold air. Don't open the door and stand there deciding what you want. Decide first, *then* open the door.

- A gasket of flexible plastic or rubber seals the crack between the door and the compartment. Place a piece of paper between the door and refrigerator cabinet. When you tug the paper, there should be a slight resistance. If not, clean the gasket or replace.

- If you're away two weeks or more, store the contents of your refrigerator and freezer with a neighbor. Clean and prop the door open. The bigger the unit, the more energy you'll save.

- Allow hot foods to cool a little bit before storing.

- Buy thermometers for your refrigerator-freezer and keep them at 38°–40°F. and at 0°F. Too cold a unit wastes energy and money.

- If the frost is more than one-quarter inch thick in the freezer, the compressor is overburdened.

<u>$$ ACTION TIP</u>: For more easy-to-follow pointers on saving money on energy, get a free copy of "Tips for Energy Savers" from CAREIRS, 800-523-2929.

## HELP FOR FINANCIALLY TROUBLED FAMILIES

If your monthly household income is less than the amounts shown in the following chart, you may be eligible for a grant to help pay heating and utility bills. The Home Energy Assistance Program (HEAP) is funded by the federal government and administered by local offices.

| Family size | Income | Family size | Income |
|---|---|---|---|
| 1 | $ 863 | 6 | $2,335 |
| 2 | 1,157 | 7 | 2,629 |
| 3 | 1,452 | 8 | 2,877 |
| 4 | 1,746 | 9 | 2,939 |
| 5 | 2,040 | 10 | 3,192 |

*To apply:* If you're under age sixty you must apply in person. Call your local utility company and ask for the location of the nearest HEAP office. Bring your current utility bill, proof of total monthly household gross income, and documents identifying each member of your household, such as birth certificates, Social Security cards, school records, and driver's licenses. Those over age sixty or disabled can apply by mail.

## KEEPING MOVING

The average American driver burns up 507 gallons of gas a year—and that pumps 11,150 pounds of carbon monoxide into our air. Increasing a car's mileage by just *one mile per gallon* cuts the amount of carbon monoxide spewed out by 528 pounds. If helping the environment doesn't convince you, take a look at this statistic: Increasing fuel efficiency by 15% will save $91 a year, or about $1,000 over the average life of a car.

Cutting back on transportation costs is also relatively simple.

- Carpool it to work. If your drive is a difficult one through lots of traffic, sharing it with several friends will make it a lot less tedious.

- Take public transportation. Leave the car at home and take the bus, train, or subway.

- Walk or bike, and encourage your children to do the same. If your kids must be driven to school or home from after-school events, form a car pool with other parents.

- Turn in your gas guzzler. Buy a fuel-efficient car.

- Keep your car well-tuned. Change oil filters every 7,500 miles and check the filters twice a year. A car in good condition uses up to 15% less gas than one that is not.

- By using less gas you're kinder and gentler to the environment, you save money, and you do your bit to make America less dependent on foreign oil.

- Drive 55. If everyone in the U.S. drove 55 mph we would save 2 million gallons of gas a day.

- Avoid excessive idling while warming up the car or waiting for friends. Today's vehicles are designed to warm up in a matter of seconds. And it takes more gas to idle your car for even a minute than to turn it off and start it again.

- Use gas with the octane level recommended by your car's manufacturer. On a national scale, this could save almost 3 million gallons of gas a day. Most new cars run best on 87 octane gas.

- Plan trips. If you have three errands to run, consolidate them into one trip. If you can, drive when traffic is at a minimum; you will get there faster and use less gas.

# WHAT CHANGING OIL PRICES MEAN

Regardless of what happens in the Middle East, Americans will remain dependent on oil—to drive our cars, heat our homes, fuel our factories, and provide a basic feedstock for the chemical industry—until truly viable alternatives are put into everyday use. We are, however, becoming more efficient: Before the last crisis, Americans consumed 266,000 metric tons of oil to generate goods and services worth $1 billion. Today it takes only 179,000 tons. Nevertheless, energy stocks should continue to do well during the recession. And even if the current Persian Gulf crisis is resolved, there could be yet another disruption, and another. Keep in mind that the price of oil was climbing before Iraq's invasion of Kuwait and that trend is likely to continue over the next several years. One way to protect yourself is by owning stocks which prosper in this environment.

## TEN RECOMMENDED ENERGY STOCKS TO HELP YOU COPE

• Arkla Inc.   (NYSE: ALG)   Price: $19*   Yield: 5.6%*

Arkla distributes natural gas to communities in Arkansas, Louisiana, and throughout the Southwest. It also produces much of its own natural gas. Earnings have continued to grow during the last five years even though the natural gas industry has been plagued by low prices. ALG's recent acquisition of Diversified Energies, Inc. will extend marketing operations into Minnesota and other northern Midwestern states. When natural gas prices rise to levels that reflect their energy-equivalent value with the price of oil, Arkla will be a major beneficiary.

---

*Prices and yields on January 7, 1991.

- Atlantic Richfield   (NYSE: ARC)   Price: $122*
  Yield: 4.1%*

For many years, ARCO has turned in outstanding financial results. Its profit margins are among the highest in the industry at all stages of its fully integrated operations. Alaskan production is declining, but foreign production is picking up the slack. ARCO owns 1.3 million acres of oil leases in Alaska which, if they prove to be productive, will give this company's future a great boost. Average oil prices of $23 per barrel will enable ARC to continue its outstanding record.

- Baker Hughes   (NYSE: BAK)   Price: $24*
  Yield: 2.0%*

BAK is a leading oil service company which has dramatically increased its earning power by acquiring Hughes Tool, the world's leading manufacturer of oil drilling bits. More recently, it acquired Eastman Christensen, a leader in the newest oil-drilling technology of horizontal and directional drilling. The markets which BAK serves are growing and will provide Baker with excellent profit margins.

- Chevron Corp.   (NYSE: CHV)   Price: $71*
  Yield: 4.4%*

Chevron, which acquired Gulf Corp. in 1984, is one of the largest international oil companies based in the U.S. It is currently undergoing a transition aimed at increasing profitability and providing the largest returns to its stockholders. Pennzoil, which also trades on the NYSE, priced at $64, owns 9% of Chevron, which lends urgency to Chevron's efforts to get results. The company has many strengths and, as management moves quickly to improve results, earnings and dividends should increase substantially.

- Consolidated Natural Gas (NYSE: CNG)    Price: $44*
  Yield: 2.4%*

The fortunes of natural gas distributors could increase as more and more people turn to this clean-burning fuel which also costs about 35% less than oil. This company has increased its oil and gas holdings in the Gulf of Mexico to 500,000+ acres and has expanded its pipelines in Ohio, Pennsylvania, and Virginia. Annual revenues are currently at $3 billion.

- Exxon Corp.    (NYSE: XON)    Price: $52*
  Yield: 5.2%*

Big is beautiful. Exxon is a leading player in all aspects of the oil industry—crude oil, natural gas, and chemicals. It has enormous financial strength and a worldwide profile. Both factors put the company in the forefront of most profit opportunities. Dividends have been raised in all but one of the last ten years.

- Halliburton    (NYSE: HAL)    Price: $44*    Yield: 2.4%*

Halliburton specializes in drilling shallow and medium gas wells. In addition, its foreign operations, which are very healthy, cover all types of oil service. It also upgrades oil refineries and builds platforms for offshore oil and gas production. The company has more cash than its total debt, which gives it a great deal of financial strength.

- Phillips Petroleum    (NYSE: P)    Price: $25*
  Yield: 4.5%*

Phillips took on an enormous debt load in 1985 to avoid a takeover. Since then, management has done an exemplary job in reducing debt from 85% of capital to a more manageable 62%. A further opportunity will arise in 1992 when Phillips will refinance $2.3 billion of debt for which they currently pay 14%. Asset values and cash flows are substantial and as debt is reduced and refinanced, shareholders will be the beneficiaries.

- Schlumberger  (NYSE: SLB)  Price: $54*
  Yield: 2.2%*

SLB is the world leader in oil reservoir information technology — it drops wires into oil wells to electronically read the presence and amounts of oil. Its newest MAXIS 500 wireline system is commanding higher prices than its older systems. Schlumberger's balance sheet is exceptionally strong. Earnings could grow at a rate in excess of 20% a year.

- Texaco  (NYSE: TX)  Price: $58*  Yield: 5.5%*

Texaco has restructured itself in the wake of its bankruptcy and has refocused the company to give it substantial earnings leverage. With crude oil priced at $23 to $26 per barrel, TX could report as much as $5.50 to $5.80 per share. Major improvements have been made and more are on the way. Every $1.00 increase in the price of crude oil adds $0.50 to the earnings per share of Texaco.

# 7

# It's Chic to Be Cheap

WELCOME to the Puritan 90s! Conspicuous consumption is out. (Naturally, marketers have replaced it with a new buzzword, "investment spending," which means buying things that we will enjoy for a long time. Since retail prices do fall in a recession, investment spending costs less!) If you have been following our advice, you've already drawn up a budget and should have a pretty good idea about where you will need to cut costs. Some areas are universals: Spending on entertaining, dining out, groceries, travel, and other consumer purchases can be easily reduced. They don't need to be cut out entirely; we will give you some specific tips in this chapter for painless ways to save.

If you don't yet have a sensible amount of money in savings, read this chapter and you can use the extra cash in your pocket to build your nest egg and to pay off debt. Even if you feel fairly comfortable, you can apply these savings to your retirement fund, children's college tuition, your investment portfolio, or to take advantage of the bargains on luxury items you will always find in a recession. You won't be alone; in the 90s it's chic to be cheap.

# THIRTY-THREE WAYS TO SAVE:
## WHEN CHEAPER IS BETTER

One nice thing about the recession is that it's now bad taste to be splashy. Even Donald Trump has been dumped by the slump. Here's a cornucopia of fashionable tips for today's world.

1. *Pump your own gas*. You will pay an average of 18 cents less per gallon for gas when you do it yourself.

2. *Take your lunch to work*. Even if lunch averages only $4 a day, that adds up to $1,000 a year. At $8 a day, it totals $2,000. Brown-bag it several times a week and put the amount you save in a savings jar.

3. *Buy at yard sales*. Get there early for the best buys.

4. *Give a yard sale*. Get money for your junk and leftovers.

5. *Order your own checks*. By ordering new checks directly from a printer rather than a bank, you can cut your costs in half. Call Current, Inc., 800-533-3973, or Checks in the Mail, 800-422-2439.

6. *Wash laundry in cold water*. Water heating accounts for up to 90% of the cost of washing clothes. A hot wash/warm rinse costs about 58 cents per load versus a cold wash/cold rinse at 3 cents per load, based on electric water heating at 7.63 cents per kilowatt hour.

7. *Reset your air conditioner*. Put the thermostat up so the room is six degrees warmer than it was last year and you will cut air-conditioning costs in half.

8. *Drive at the speed limit*. When you drive 70 mph instead of 55, your fuel loss can be as much as 35%. That means a gallon of gas for which you paid $1.20 actually cost you $1.62.

9. *Quit smoking*. If you smoke one pack a day at $2 a pack, by kicking the habit you can save $730 in one year.

According to GEICO, your life insurance costs will be just about half that of a smoker.

10. *Clip food coupons*. If you save $15 a month with product coupons, that's $180 a year. If you shop for a family, you could save $15 a week, which will give you an annual savings of $780.

11. *Circumvent expensive college visits*. Although a personal visit to an out-of-state campus is nice for a college-bound student, it is expensive. The next best thing is a videotape tour. Collegiate Choice, 41 Surrey Lane, Tenafly, NJ 07670, 201-871-0098, has more than 275 student-guided campus tours on tape. They run between twenty and ninety minutes and cost $20 for one tour and $15 for each additional tour. You can also band together with other parents and share the purchase price.

12. *Car insurance discounts* are often available for commuters who carpool it to work . . . also for cars driven only by a woman, and for cars equipped with antitheft devices. Ask your agent.

13. *Share newspapers with your coworkers*. If you buy the *Wall Street Journal* and the *New York Times* every weekday, you're spending $299 per year. Share them with three office-mates and you will save $100.

14. *Shop for banks*. These days, banks have all sorts of creative ways to charge you for their services. Some charge a monthly fee, a fee per check or per use of an ATM machine, or even a combination of the two. Many times account fees are waived if you keep a minimum balance, but you will have to calculate whether you would earn more money investing that amount in a CD or money market fund.

15. *Take your old clothes to the tailor*. The old adage is true: Hemlines rise during a recession. But fashion's fads are costly. For $15 to $50 you can reshape your old clothes

to appear stylishly new and save hundreds of dollars in replacement costs.

16. *Buy your phone*. A year ago, AT&T raised its rates on leased phones from 25 cents to 95 cents per month. A basic touch-tone model jumped from $4.25 a month or $51 a year, to $5.10 a month or $62 a year. Comparable phones can be purchased for $50 or less.

17. *Sew again*. Follow "Today" host Deborah Norville's example and save money by sewing your own clothes, curtains, etc. You can still be chic: Fashion designer Carolyne Roehm has a line of patterns for Vogue. If you need lessons, call the American Home Sewing & Craft Association's toll-free number for class referrals: 800-U-SEW-NOW.

18. *Slash stockbroker's fees*: Use a discount broker, such as Charles Schwab (800-435-4000), Quick & Reilly (800-221-5220), or Muriel Siebert & Co. (800-872-0711), and save over 50% when buying or selling stocks, bonds, and some mutual funds. An alternative is to ask your full-service broker to give you a discount. Times are tough on Wall Street; you might be able to negotiate.

19. *Talk is cheap*. If most of your telephone calls are to a single area code, check out AT&T's SelectSaver plan and get reduced rates.

20. *Talk can be cheaper*. Regular long-distance calls made after 5 P.M. generally cost 4 to 10 cents less per minute than calls made before 5 P.M. on weekdays. Calling after 11 P.M. or on a weekend saves another 2 to 3 cents per minute.

21. *Invest in a good home-repair guide*. Not only will it save you the cost of outside help, but many of us are accustomed to throwing things away when they're broken due to the high cost of repairs. But a torn screen can be

mended, it need not be replaced; and most spots and stains *can* be removed.

22. *Buy stamps at the post office.* If you order stamps by phone using a credit card, there's a $3 fee. At convenience stores you can wind up paying 40 cents for a 25-cent stamp.

23. *Join a club.* Money-saving clubs exist for a variety of purchases, from air travel to discounted theater tickets. The national book chains, Walden and B. Dalton, both offer discount savings after you've reached a certain level of purchases. So does HMV on records, tapes, and compact discs.

24. *Subscribe to magazines.* If you regularly read a magazine, it pays to subscribe. A subscription to *Lear's*, for example, is only $18, while twelve copies bought at the newstand at $3 each is $36.

25. *Get a warranty on dental work.* If you pay at least half of your dental bills with OPT 4, a dental credit card (800-247-0157), you won't be charged if bridges, crowns, or caps need fixing within five months. The card has a one-time fee of $20 and a high interest rate: 19.8%. So make sure you pay off your balance promptly.

26. *Don't buy clothes that need dry cleaning.*

27. *Buy a car in December.* Just before Christmas is a slow time for auto dealers plus they want to unload that year's models. Negotiate tough. Worst time to buy: March through June, when people plan their summer vacations.

28. *Get your money back.* If you're having trouble with a new appliance and neither the authorized repair dealer nor the manufacturer is responding, contact the Major Appliance Consumer Action Panel for help: Call 800-621-0477, or write to 20 North Wacker Drive, Chicago, IL 60606.

29. _Limit the amount of cash you carry_. If you leave your checkbook and your credit cards at home, you won't be _able_ to spend your money.

30. _If you work for yourself, get the breaks you deserve_. Look into the many benefits available from membership in the National Association for the Self-Employed (NASE). Members get discounts on office products, business cards, travel, rental cars, etc., as well as group health and dental insurance. Contact NASE at 2328 Gravel Road, Fortworth, TX 76118; 800-232-NASE.

31. _Don't pay twice what paper's worth_. Check out Staples, the "Office Superstore." With sixty-eight stores nationwide, they offer deep discounts on office products and furniture. Average prices are 50% off list. To find the store nearest you call the company headquarters in Newton, Massachusetts: 617-969-3901.

32. _Beat the cost of paying a baby-sitter_. Set up a co-op service with friends and neighbors. Detailed instructions are given by Marguerite Kelly in her book _Mother's Almanac III_ (New York: Doubleday; $12.95).

33. _Get a low-rate credit card_. Banks, not credit cards, set their own interest rates and annual fees. For an up-to-date list of banks offering no-fee credit cards, or a list of banks offering low-interest credit cards, send $1.50 per category to: Bankcard Holders of America, 560 Herndon Parkway, Suite 120, Herndon, VA 22070. For an additional $1, get "How to Choose a Credit Card."

$$ ACTION TIP: _Insure your cash_. If you bank at a federally insured institution—one which has a FDIC (Federal Deposit Insurance Corporation) sign displayed, you're automatically insured up to $100,000. But only individual depositors, not individual accounts, are insured, _including_ interest and principal. If you have three accounts in the same name in one bank, you are insured _only_ for a total of $100,000, not

$300,000. However, if you are married, you and your spouse can insure up to $500,000 at one bank by establishing several types of accounts: two individual accounts, one for each of you; a joint account; and two testamentary revocable trusts, one set up for each of you. This type of account pays the balance to the beneficiary upon the death of the trustee. You can also set up joint accounts with children and get additional coverage. For a free brochure on how FDIC insurance works, call the FDIC at 800-424-5488.

## NEW WAYS TO ENTERTAIN

In times of recession, splashy parties are an example of conspicuous consumption at its worst. Some of your friends have lost their jobs and others have had to cut back on spending. Or you may be the one who has lost the job or whose business is suffering. At any rate, it's not the time to spend wild amounts on lavish parties. Here are a few terrific ideas for being chic on the cheap.

- *Do it yourself.* Don't let tradition, habit, or lack of experience drive you into the arms of a fancy caterer. Do your own cooking or, if neither you nor your spouse or friends are good cooks, then try the next suggestion. (If you are a caterer, investigate ways to save money, and pass on the savings to your clients!)
- *Give a potluck dinner.* This old Midwestern custom is a great money- and time-saver. When you invite friends for dinner, tell them it's potluck—that is, each person is bringing part of the meal—the hors d'oeuvres, soup, main dish, salad, dessert. As the host, you may wish to prepare the main dish or provide the cocktails, wine, and coffee. You may start a new trend in your town.
- *Give a theme party.* You don't need to provide a four-course dinner every time you entertain. Invite friends over

for cocktails, or serve wine and cheese or sandwiches and coffee while watching the Superbowl on television. Have people come by for coffee and dessert after a concert, the school play, football game, or other community event.

- *Keep it simple*. Fortunately, the most fashionable foods today are the least expensive and the healthiest. Pasta, vegetables, and rice are replacing the more expensive roast beef, chops, and steak of the past.

- *Keep the drinking cheap*. Americans are switching from hard liquor to wine—a move that makes entertaining easier on the pocketbook. Inexpensive but good wines are very much in vogue, so don't let a wine snob talk you into serving an outrageously pricey wine. Instead, serve California, New York State, Spanish, or Chilean wines. Read the wine reviews in the paper or *Gourmet* magazine, and don't be shy about serving good domestic and foreign beers, sparkling water, and diet sodas.

## DINING OUT FOR LESS

There are some pretty obvious ways to cut back—one is to eat at home and the other is to dine at less expensive restaurants. Yet we all crave a candlelit dinner at a nice restaurant now and then, even in the worst of times. So here are some less obvious ways to trim the fat from the bill:

*Rule 1.* Have cocktails at home. Alcoholic beverages in a restaurant are expensive, so invite friends to join you for cocktails at your home and then go on to dinner.

*Rule 2.* If you do drink at a restaurant, do so in moderation. Order just one cocktail or glass of wine. And, always ask the price. Many restaurants have a less expensive house wine as well as one or two other more expensive wines sold by the glass.

*Rule 3.* Ethnic foods are cheaper (and often better) than the more traditional European or American fare. Try Mexican,

Chinese, Japanese, Thai, Indian, and Pakistani foods. You can also get these to take out and serve at home to a crowd. And don't overlook pizzas and pastas, which with a salad make a great cheap meal.

*Rule 4*. If the menu is à la carte, then skip the appetizer and have dessert or vice versa. Or serve dessert and coffee at home.

*Rule 5*. Eat breakfast or lunch out instead of dinner; both are 50% to 85% less expensive than dinner.

*Rule 6*. Take advantage of "early bird specials." These dinners, typically served from 4 P.M. to 6 P.M., are substantially cheaper, yet it's the same food, and the same atmosphere.

*Rule 7*. Always add up the check yourself. Harried waiters make honest mistakes and sometimes dishonest mistakes, especially in large cities. Bring a pencil, and a pocket calculator if you're not a math whiz. Add in the tip carefully. The rule of thumb for good service is 12–15% of the total check. In states where there's a a 6–8% tax, you can double the tax for quick figuring. Poor service need not be rewarded but should be pointed out to the manager.

$$ ACTION TIP: You can pay 20% less for many restaurant meals by using a special credit card that provides discounts. For information, contact:

- Advantage Charge Trading            (212-779-SAVE)
  Corp. (ACT)
  114 East 32 Street
  New York, NY 10016

- Transmedia Network Inc.            (800-422-5090)
  11900 Biscayne Boulevard
  North Miami, FL 33181


Before signing on, ask for a list of participating restaurants and be sure to find out if there is an annual fee; if the discount is restricted on certain days, hours, or menu items; if it covers tip and tax; and when you should show your card—upon entry or when you are finished eating. In some situations you may be limited as to how many people may accompany you.

## THE BUDGET GOURMET

These days it's easy to walk out of the supermarket with two bags of groceries and $50 less in your wallet. The average American family spends 15% of their after-tax income on food. But you and your family have to eat, and there are many ways to cut down on expenses and still enjoy delicious meals!

Try the following ideas:

1. Join a food co-op. Discounts for members range from 5% to 20% because items are packaged in bulk.
2. Comparison shop. Not all supermarkets charge the same amounts for the same items.
3. Stay away from convenience stores; prices are 15–45% higher.
4. Stews and pot roasts, because they are cooked a long time, enable you to use cheaper cuts of meat, such as chuck.
5. Use day-old bread and rolls for making stuffings, bread puddings, or French toast.
6. Overripe fruit is excellent in muffins and breads.
7. Use coupons!

## FIX-UP INSTEAD OF TRADE UP

One of the first casualties of this recession has been real estate. Throughout the country, prices of homes, condos, and urban cooperative apartments have been hit hard—in many cases they have fallen 20–30% of their former values. Under the circumstances, it's usually best to stay put until the real estate picture gets rosier. But while waiting, *improve* your home, doing the things you've always wanted. If you can do it yourself so much the better, but if not, you will find plenty of experienced contractors and workmen anxious for work and available at reasonable prices.

Most improvements will pay off when it is time to sell. Adding to the value of your house can be as simple as applying a coat of fresh paint or as complicated as adding a new room. Before picking up a hammer or getting out the stepladder, look to see if you need basic repairs such as plumbing, new windows, or replacement of worn-out fixtures. If so, do these first. Then, when you do your renovations, don't spend over 20% of the value of the house on remodeling or upgrading. If you need to borrow money for a renovation, use your home as a financing tool; interest on home equity loans is tax-deductible. (See Chapter 5 on borrowing.) The three areas of greatest return are improvements to kitchens, bathrooms, and master bedroom suites.

**$$ ACTION TIP**: Before starting, consult *A Consumer's Guide to Home Improvement, Renovation, & Repair* (New York, John Wiley & Sons, 1990; $19.95), at your library.

Some improvements pay off immediately. If you or someone in your family is running a business from home, consider putting in an official home office. Not only will it be useful, there are also tax advantages. The IRS allows you to deduct certain office expenses if the office is used exclusively on a regular basis as your principal place of business or as a place in which patients, clients, or customers meet or deal with you in the normal course of your business. This tax break is usually not extended to employees. Keep receipts for telephone, utilities, insurance, rental costs, taxes, depreciation, maintenance, security system, etc. You may need to provide physical evidence of an office: A desk, chair, and filing cabinet is the bare minimum. Order the free IRS pamphlet #587, "Business Use of Your Home," for all the facts.

$$ ACTION TIP: Barter. If you're a klutz with a tool kit, or you don't even own one, make a trade. Ask a more experienced neighbor to help and in exchange, do something for him.

CAUTION: Most states offer consumers very little help if a dispute with a contractor arises on home improvement projects. Take these steps on your own when hiring a contractor:

1. Call the bank and Better Business Bureau to check on the contractor's reputation. One of the biggest problems is that contractors sometimes go bankrupt before they finish the job.

2. Ask if he has workers' compensation insurance; otherwise you are liable if someone is hurt on your job. If you hire free-lance or moonlighting carpenters or other workers, they probably won't have workers' compensation or general liability insurance. Check to see that your home owner's insurance will cover any injuries on your property.

3. Have permits taken out in the contractor's name; if the job doesn't pass muster with the local inspector of meet city requirements, it will be his responsibility, not yours.

4. Get a warranty for at least one year and if possible, an extended five-year warranty to cover structural problems.

5. Stagger your payments, with 10–20% up front and small installments as the work is completed. Hold off on the last payment until the work has been approved by you.

6. Don't hire someone who won't take a check.

7. Always have a written contract. For a copy of a standard home improvement contract, write to the American Homeowners Foundation, 1724 South Quincy Street, Arlington, VA 22204 (703-979-4663). The cost is $5.95.

## BUY-IT-YOURSELF SERVICES

Home centers—those huge outlets where you can buy everything from bathtubs to storm windows—are starting to offer a buy-it-yourself option: you buy the tub and the store will supply a skilled plumber to install it for you. The savings is about 15% off the standard contractor's price. On simpler projects, such as putting up a fence or laying a carpet, you can save even more. Stores with the buy-it-yourself plan include Hechinger (113 stores nationwide); Home Depot (127 stores); Builders Square, a division of K Mart (146 stores); Channel Home Centers (86 stores); and Sears' 800-outlet Home Improvement Products & Services (HIPs).

## FASHIONS FOR LESS

Is there a secret to buying clothes for less? You can shop the sales, of course, but the biggest bargains are found at discount stores, outlet malls, and off-price chains. Once you're on the scene, having the instincts of a Middle Eastern rug merchant will help you root out the best bargains. You will find brand-name items at markdowns ranging from 20 to 70%.

Before you go, review these three rules:

*Rule 1.* Don't shop with a list of things you absolutely must buy. When you find them, you will buy them regardless of the price. Instead, keep a general shopping list of items you feel you need to acquire *if* they are available in the right size and color and at the right price. Assign a dollar cap to each item and don't go above it.

*Rule 2.* Don't let social pressures, mostly imaginary, force you into the must-buy category. If the kids need new sneakers and you can't find hand-me-downs, hold off until you see a good sale or can get to an outlet store. Buying name-brand sneakers because your children say, "All the other kids have them" is lunacy. In the words of Nancy Reagan, "Just say no."

*Rule 3.* Don't be seduced by designer labels. It may be designed by someone famous but it could look terrible on you.

## WHERE THE OUTLETS ARE

| State | Town |
| --- | --- |
| Alabama | Boaz, Foley |
| California | Gilroy, Pacific Grove, South Lake Tahoe, Vacaville |
| Colorado | Silverthorne |
| Connecticut | Branford, East Windsor, Milford, Mystic, Norwalk |
| Delaware | Rehoboth |
| Florida | Orlando |
| Georgia | Commerce |
| Illinois | St. Charles |
| Indiana | Michigan City |
| Maine | Freeport, Kittery |
| Maryland | Annapolis, Perrysville, Queenstown |
| Massachusetts | Buzzards Bay, Lawrence, Lenox, New Bedford, Plymouth |
| Michigan | Birch Run, Holland, Monroe |
| Missouri | Branson, Osage Beach |
| New Hampshire | Keene, North Conway, West Lebanon, Manchester |
| New Jersey | Flemington, Secaucus |
| New York | Central Valley, Lake George, Latham, Monticello, Niagara Falls, Plattsburgh, Saratoga |

| | |
|---|---|
| North Carolina | Blowing Rock, Brighton, Burlington, Smithfield |
| Ohio | Aurora, Sandusky |
| Pennsylvania | Lancaster, Reading, York |
| South Carolina | Hilton Head, Santee |
| Tennessee | Chattanooga, Pigeon Forge |
| Texas | Conroe, Hillsboro, New Braunfels, Sulphur Springs |
| Vermont | Manchester |
| Virginia | Virginia Beach, Waynesboro, Williamsburg |
| Washington | Burlington |
| West Virginia | Martinsburg |
| Wisconsin | Kenosha |

NOTE: Two chains specializing in off-price clothing, which have stores throughout the U.S., are Loehmann's (73 stores) and Syms (27 stores).

---

\$\$ ACTION TIP: Consult *Joy of Outlet Shopping*, available for \$3.95 from Outlet Consumer Reporter, Box 7876, St. Petersburg, FL 33734; or call the toll-free outlet hot line, Outlet Bound, 800-336-8853, to find the outlets in your area. Another excellent reference is the *Factory Outlet Guide to New England* available for \$8.95, plus \$2 for shipping and handling, from Globe Pequot Press, 138 West Main Street, Chester, CT 06412.

You should of course take advantage of store sales. And when the economy is in trouble, there are more and more sales. If you have a charge card—which you're not using during the recession—you will receive advance notice of special sales. Arrive early but don't get swept away in the frantic madness that accompanies these events. Instead, go, look, decide, buy, and leave. *Thrift shops* run by charities and *vintage clothing stores*, such as Cheap Jack's in New York, are very inexpensive and fun to browse in. *Army-navy stores* have good-quality surplus military clothing at reasonable prices as well as shoes, sneakers, socks, hats, coats, parkas, blankets, sleeping bags, and camping equipment.

Catalog shopping can also offer significant discounts.

## SHOP BY MAIL FOR BIG DISCOUNTS

Whether you're looking for a coat or a cocktail outfit, a suit or a layette set, you can save on gasoline or footwork by shopping from home. Savings are often 50% or more. Here are some of the best in fashion bargains. For more ideas, read *The Wholesale-By-Mail Catalog* by Lowell Miller and Prudence McCullough, New York: Harper & Row, 1991. The cost is $12.95. Or, for $14.95, *America By Mail*, New York: Avon, 1990.

| | |
|---|---|
| • Chadwick's of Boston, Ltd.<br>1 Chadwick Place<br>Box 1600<br>Brockton, MA 02403<br>508-583-6600 | Women's clothing and accessories |
| • Lee-McClain Co., Inc.<br>Route 6<br>Box 381A<br>Shelbyville, KY 40065<br>502-633-3823 | Men's business clothing |
| • Land's End, Inc.<br>Dodgeville, WI 53595-0001<br>800-356-4444 | Work and weekend clothing for men, women, and children |
| • National Wholesale Co., Inc.<br>400 National Blvd.<br>Lexington, NC 27294<br>704-249-0211 | Women's hosiery, underwear |

- Paul Fredrick Shirt Co.          Men's dress shirts
  140 West Main Street
  Fleetwood, PA 19522
  800-247-1417

- Rubens & Marble, Inc.          Infant's clothes and
  Box 14900                            bedding
  Chicago, IL 60614-0900
  312-348-6200

- The Hanover Shoe Co.          Men's shoes; some
  118 Carlisle Street                   women's
  Hanover, PA 17331
  800-426-3708

- Okun Bros. Shoes               Shoes for men and
  356 East South Street              women
  Kalamazoo, MI 49007
  800-433-6344

## WAREHOUSE BONANZA

A new shopping phenomenon, no-frills warehouses located on the outskirts of towns, offer some of the best recession shopping. They are only open to members, who typically pay a yearly fee of between $25–$35. Two leaders are the Price Club (with warehouses in over ten states and Canada), and Sam's Club, owned by Wal-Mart. These warehouses act primarily as wholesalers, selling food, office supplies, and other necessities at prices about 8% above the manufacturer's cost.

Warehouse-sized supermarkets, like Cub Foods and Omni Super Stores, are "bag your own" operations with minimum service and maximum discounts for foods (but no produce), some clothing, appliances, stationery, toys, etc. For the best and cheapest in home furnishings, try IKEA (rhymes with idea), which has eighty-eight stores worldwide. You can drop off the kids in the store's free supervised play area while you shop for kitchen cabinets, living room furniture, book-cases, etc., at enormous discounts. (IKEA won *Money* magazine's "Store of the year" award in 1990.)

## BARGAIN TRAVEL AND VACATIONS

At home and abroad, the cost of air travel is sky-high, thanks largely to the soaring price of fuel. Paring costs is increasingly critical to having a good time, whether it's a business trip, family vacation, or solo sojourn. Begin by locking in fares now, well in advance of your trip, since more rate hikes are expected to cover spiraling jet fuel costs during the recession.

That's the bad news. The good news is that the surge in oil prices has forced nervous operators and packagers to woo travelers with discounts on fly/drive packages, rooms, and airline/hotel deals. And certain types of travel are actually becoming less outrageously expensive because of the recession—travel within the U.S., Latin America, and Canada is more reasonable than to Europe and the Far East, for instance. Many cruise lines are slashing prices.

But don't kid yourself. It's still going to cost more than staying home. Here are some ways to travel cheaper and still be chic.

## HOW TO GET REAL DISCOUNTS

• Begin by subscribing to *Travel Smart*, a monthly newsletter (Communications House, 40 Beechdale Road, Dobbs Ferry, NY 10522; 800-327-3633, in New York State, 914-693-8300; $44 a year, with a $37 introductory offer) that tracks the best in travel deals, both domestic and foreign. Subscribers can book the lowest airfares, hotel rooms, packages, and cruises through the newsletter's special number: 914-427-0269.

• *Be a Courier*. If you're flexible about departure and

arrival dates, you can save up to two thirds of the price of round-trip tickets to major U.S. and foreign cities by being a courier. A courier carries business documents, such as canceled checks, blueprints, or legal papers, for an individual or a company. On foreign flights, part of the deal is waiting for the package to pass through customs. Although it's a cheap way to travel, there are some disadvantages: Couriers must travel light, since the delivery company uses the personal baggage allowance for its packages; the length of your stay may be restricted; and if you're not going solo, your friends or family will have to pay full fare.

$$ ACTION TIP: Check the yellow pages or one of these air courier agencies at least a month before you plan to travel: • Way To Go Travel Club in Hollywood, California: 213-851-2572; • Jupiter Air in Los Angeles: 213-670-5123; • Now Voyager in New York City: 212-431-1616; • World Courier in Brooklyn, NY: 718-978-9408.

• *Check out company discounts.* If you work for a medium-to large-sized company, you may be eligible for a company discount. Many firms have their own travel department or use an agency on a regular basis and can negotiate lower rates with hotels and car-rental agencies. These discounts are often available for employees' personal trips.

• *Shop for traveler's checks.* Some banks provide traveler's checks free to preferred customers. But you have to ask. Then when possible, cash them at the issuers' bank or outlet since most issuers do not charge for cashing their own checks. For example, Barclays' Visa checks are cashed free at U.K. Barclays Banks, while American Express does the same at its American Express outlets, and, for corporate clients, Thomas Cook at its own offices.

• *Senior citizens (sixty-two and older) get some of the best travel deals.* Ask for information on Eastern Airlines' Get-Up-and-Go Passport and Travel Pass, and TWA's Senior Travel Pak. If you're sixty-two or older it's always worthwhile to mention your age when making inquiries into air, train, or bus travel. Chances are you will be eligible for some sort of discount.

• *Join a last-minute-travel club*. These members-only clubs offer discounts of 50% or more on the price of packaged tours, hotel rooms, and cruises. The disadvantage is that you can't plan a trip more than two weeks in advance. Moment's Notice in New York City, one of the best-known, has been operating since 1981. Call 212-486-0500. Moment's Notice also offers reduced prices on some individual domestic and foreign airline tickets and hotel rooms. Membership is $45 a year and includes the hot line number to call for last-minute destinations and discounts.

Last Minute Travel in Boston, Massachusetts, offers a taped hotline, not toll-free, and a monthly newsletter which gives specials. Call 800-527-8646. Last Minute Cruise Club in San Pedro, California, buys blocks of tickets from cruise lines and resells them at discount. They send a newsletter with those available but there is no toll-free hotline. Call 213-519-1717.

• *Insure your trip*. When booking an expensive trip or one to an area with political problems, cancellation insurance can provide some peace of mind. It reimburses otherwise nonrefundable deposits if the packager defaults or you need to back out for a good cause—illness or a death in the family, for instance. Insurance is also sold to cover medical emergencies and loss of personal belongings, but these are usually covered by medical and home owners' policies, so check your policy first. The major insurers are: • Access America (Empire and Capital Area Blue Cross and Blue Shield) in New York: 800-284-8300; • Tele-Trip Company (Mutual of Omaha) in Omaha, NB: 800-228-9792; • Travel Guard International (CIGNA Insurance) in Stevens Point, Wisconsin: 800-826-1300; and • Travel Insurance Pak (The Travelers) in Hartford, Connecticut: 800-243-3174.

• *Get the most out of your dollar abroad*. The value of the U.S. dollar vis-à-vis foreign currencies changes daily. Current exchange rates are listed in the *Wall Street Journal*, or call Deak International at 800-368-5683. Details on a foreign country's restrictions are available from its embassy in Washington, DC. In most cases the exchange rate is more favorable *within the country* because of competition among foreign exchange dealers; and the best rates are almost always found at banks, not at hotels, airports, or shops.

• *Other dollar savers:* • Avoid making a series of small exchanges because fees cut into the principal. • Take $100 in foreign currency (for tips and getting from the airport to the hotel, etc.), the rest in U.S. dollar–denominated traveler's checks to convert as you move from one country to another. This avoids the problem of converting British pounds into French francs and French francs into Italian lira as you make your way across Europe. You'll wind up paying exchange fees several times. • If you live in a small town, give your bank several weeks' notice to get the currency in time. • As you reach your destination, cash traveler's checks only as you need them. You want to avoid leaving the country with lots of foreign cash—converting back to dollars can be very expensive.

• *When the dollar is rising:* • Buy traveler's checks in dollars. • Don't change all the dollars you plan to spend when you first arrive. • Pay with a credit or charge card so you'll be billed later. (A credit card purchase made abroad is converted into U.S. dollars when the charge is posted, not on the day the item is purchased.)

• *When the dollar is falling:* • Exchange dollars into the foreign currency as soon as possible, though generally not before leaving the U.S. • Buy traveler's checks in foreign currency. • Book prepaid tours and packages that have guaranteed prices. • Limit your use of your credit card.

## SIX SUPER SAVERS

There are as many ways to save while you travel as there are varying fares within the airline industry: In other words, a lot. And like the wide range of airfares to the same destination, finding the best deal can be a bit confusing. During a recession it pays to research and explore as many of them as possible. You will find helpful hints in travel magazines, and chances are your friends will share their bargain strategies with you, but here are six tips to get you started:

1. *Clip ads* for airline, hotel, and car rental discount offers and bring them with you to the reservation desk. It's best to bring the whole page, including the name of the publication and the date. Management often advertises specials and off-season deals but neglects to tell front-office employees of the reduced prices.

2. *Become your own travel agent.* For those who travel frequently, it's worthwhile to sign up for a travel reservation system that serves personal computer owners. Using a modem and phone, you call up the system, enter a user code, and get access to airline schedules, fares, and on-time performances. You can beat everyone else to the lowest fares, reserve your flight and seat, charge your ticket, and get it by mail. The most comprehensive service is the *Official Airline Guide* (OAG), electronic edition. Subscribers pay up to 47 cents a minute from 6:01 PM until 8:00 AM, when the rate drops to 17 cents a minute. But if you enter a reservation, it's free. Call 800-323-3537 for details. The OAG system is also available through CompuServe. Also check: Eaasy (yes, two a's) Sabre system available for computer users through Prodigy or CompuServe. Call 800-433-7556 extension 4805. For those without computers, the OAG *Pocket Flight Guide* is $14.50; twelve issues cost $65 plus $7 handling and shipping.

3. *Show your age.* Senior discounts for those over fifty are not always advertised, so carry proof of your age with you. Some establishments require a senior citizen membership card from an organization such as Medicare or AARP, although a driver's license or passport is often enough.

4. *Seek lower hotel rates.* The standard posted price for a hotel room is called the "rack" rate. Lower rates are sometimes available if you ask when making reservations. Most major hotels and hotel chains offer a "corporate" rate, typically a 10 to 50% discount. If you can show a business card or company ID, you may qualify. An airline's frequent flyer plan usually includes participating hotels. If you are a member of an auto or oil company travel club, your card may get you a discount at certain chains. Business travelers keep rooms filled at big city hotels Monday through Thursday. On Friday night these hotels will be glad to see you, and may offer you rooms at a significant discount. Plan holiday excursions to cities where hotels offer weekend specials. These are well-advertised in the travel section of city newspapers.

5. *Get the best airfare.* Use a competent travel agency on a regular basis. Agents work harder for regular clients. The agent should have a direct access computer system—one that gives him information on available discount seats directly form the airline. He should also use one of the new computer programs that automatically search several times a day for cheaper seats, right up until twenty-four hours before your departure. Some large travel agency chains, such as Ask Mr. Foster and Thomas Cook, do a free daily computer search of airline reservation systems to see if a cheaper seat has become available. Ask your agent to do the same.

6. *Buy tickets from a consolidator.* These airfare discounters have been operating legally in the U.S. since airline deregulation in 1978. They purchase blocks of tickets from airlines and resell them at a discount to travelers. There are approximately 100 consolidators, mostly specializing in foreign travel, but some sell domestic tickets. They're still getting bad press, left over from their previously troubled days, yet the good ones are *good*. Nevertheless, pay by credit card just in case the consolidator or airline should go under. They offer 20 to 50% off normal prices to travel agents. CAUTION: Tickets are usually nonrefundable and flight times cannot be

changed. Also, most won't tell you which airline you'll be flying on. We've listed three of the best below, but if you're uncomfortable, deal with a travel agent or *Travel Smart*, listed at the beginning of this section. • Council Charter in New York City: 800-223-7402; • Travac in NYC, Los Angeles, San Francisco, and Orlando: 800-872-8800; and • UniTravel of St. Louis: 800-325-2222.

$$ ACTION TIP: *Trading places*. One way not to pay a hotel bill and still have a great vacation is to swap homes with someone else, either here or abroad. It calls for a sense of adventure and tends to be most popular with families, teachers, and others who can take long vacations. Place a classified ad in an up-market magazine such as *The New Republic*, *The Atlantic*, or *The New York Review of Books*, or others that carry home/exchange ads. To reach the international set, use the *International Herald Tribune*, published in Paris. Call 800-882-2884. New York residents may phone 212-752-3890. The most popular method of swapping is through home exchange agencies and directories: • Vacation Exchange Club, Box 820, Haleiwa, Hawaii 96712: 800-638-3841; • International Home Exchange Service in San Francisco: 415-435-3497; • Better Homes & Travel in NYC: 212-349-5340.

## TRAVEL WITH KIDS

Humorist Robert Benchley said there are two kinds of travel: "First class or with children." But that distinction need not be. You and your children can find plenty to do, ranging from first class to cheap. First-class trips are easy to find but hard to finance during a recession. Here are some cheaper ideas that hold the promise of fun for both generations:

• *Farm and ranch family vacations*. Sleep in a farmhouse, milk cows, and gather eggs. Throughout the country, paying guests can live on a farm for a weekend or longer. Rates are very reasonable. Contact state departments of agriculture and consult Pat Dickerman's *Farm, Ranch & Country Vacations*, a 229-page book which is frequently updated, and is available at your library.

• *Consider a cruise.* A number of cruise lines provide counselors for youngsters, arts and crafts workshops, gym, and organized shore trips. With bookings down, it has become far less expensive than in the past, although it's not as cheap as a farm/ranch vacation. Avoid the Christmas holiday and you'll find rates are 10 to 40% less. Check out Admiral Cruises (800-327-0271), Carnival Cruise Lines (800-327-7276), Chandris Fantasy Cruises (800-621-3446), and Dolphin Cruise Lines (800-222-1003).

For other ideas, consult: • *Family Travel Times*, 80 Eighth Avenue, New York, NY 10011; 212-206-0688. For $35 a year this newsletter covers all types of trips including those that are "eminently affordable." • Let's Take the Kids (800-726-4349) is a subscription service that provides information, advice, and specially designed tours for members. Annual membership is $35, and includes a toll-free hot line and a quarterly newsletter.

## TAKING CHILDREN ON BUSINESS TRIPS

According to the U.S. Travel Data Center, nearly one in seven business trips now includes children. It's an easy way to add on a mini-vacation, with your airfare already paid. Or, if you're a single parent, it may be easier to have your child with you than to arrange for care at home. Many hotels, conference centers, and resorts provide baby-sitter services, bonded nannies, and activities for the kids. • Sitters Unlimited (800-328-1191, 714-752-2366) runs a network of child-care helpers for traveling families, operating in a number of cities. • Hyatt Hotels (800-233-1234) has Camp Hyatt programs at fourteen conference centers and resorts that include daylong activities for children ages three to fifteen. • Marriott (800-228-9290) has mini-vacations at resort properties with weekend discounts for families and supervised programs for five- to twelve- year-olds.

## FAMILIES IN THE SUMMERTIME

Childhood memories for all of us are often of our summer days. These need not be extravagant times—yours probably weren't—but they do need to be structured, with children spending time with their parents and time on their own. One of the best on-their-own experiences is summer camp. The costs can be extravagant—several thousand dollars for a private sleep-away camp, or modest—several hundred dollars for Girl or Boy Scout camp. Church camps and other non-profit organizations, like the Y, are economical solution. For a list of camps accredited by the American Camping Association, write to their headquarters at 5000 State Street; 67 North Martinsville, IN 46151. Parents can call 800-428-CAMP for the phone number of the association's regional office nearest them. Regional offices offer a service to help callers find an accredited camp within their budget.

# Epilogue

Now that you have finished reading "How to Survive & Thrive in the Recession of 1991," you realize that our economy is cyclical and that what goes up must come down and vice versa. In other words, this recession—like all other recessions—will not last forever. Most likely it will only last a year. Remember, the first rules to follow in a recession are:

- Don't panic.
- Don't procrastinate.
- Get your finances in shape *today*.

Information is your best weapon. So begin now—if you haven't already—to implement the various $$ ACTION TIPS we've given. Not only will you handle any difficulties that come your way, you will avert a great number.

If you manage your personal finances with the following recommendations in mind, at the very least you can survive—and may thrive—during the economic slowdown.

- Prepare a budget and *stick to it*.
- Accumulate the savings you need to survive unemployment.

- Trim any fat from your day-to-day living expenses.
- Pay attention to the economic news in order to protect your savings and investments.
- Be a smart borrower.
- Protect your job by giving more than 100%.

Based on your new understanding of the business cycle, you know that the best time to prepare for the next economic boom is now, during the recession.

- If the funds are available, take advantage of the low prices in real estate.
- Be a smart investor.

Remember that the advice given in this book does not apply only to *recessionary* times. Sound financial planning will help you in all economic phases—boom or bust. And finding new ways to save is just as valuable in times of expansion. It gives you the extra funds needed to take advantage of investment opportunities.

# Index

"Adam Smith's Money World," 12, 13
Adjustable rate mortgages (ARMs): *See* Mortgages
American Stock Exchange, 34
Amos, Wally, 92
Antiques: *See* Collectibles
Appraisals:
   real property, 41
A-rated bonds, 35
Auctions, residential, 41
Auto loans, 124, 128

"Baby Bell" companies, 65
Bankruptcy, declaring personal, 145–146
   types of, 146
   Chapter 7 bankruptcy, 146
   Chapter 13 bankruptcy, 146
Banks, obtaining financial evaluation of, 29
*Barron's*, 69
Benefits, employee: *See* Employee benefits
Bills, paying your, 17–18
Blue-chip stocks: *See* Stocks
Bonds, 28, 32, 34–35, 36, 43–44
   A-rated bonds, 35
   "call provision," 35
   definition, 36
   EE savings bonds, 36
     college education, financing, 143–144
   existing bonds, 43
   expanding economy's effect on, 53–54
   face value of, 35
   faltering economy, effect of, 56
   interest rates, 43–44, 45, 56
     risk, avoiding, 35
   intermediate length bonds, short to, 35
   maturity, 35
   purchasing, 18
   recovering economy, effect of, 53–54
   selling, 35
   short to intermediate length bonds, 35
   Treasury bonds, 31, 36, 69
   war, effect of, 51
   *see also* Recession-resistant industries
Brokerage loans, 129–130
Brokers, discount, 20, 166
Budgets, 22–26, 163–174
   fixed expenses, 23
   food, cutting expenses on, 172
   monthly income, 22
   totalling expenses, 26
   unemployed, budgeting yourself when, 84–87
   variable expenses, 24
   worksheets, 22–26
   *see also* Expenses
Business cycle, 3
   expansion in, effect of, 58
   starting point, 3
   terms describing aspect of, 5–12
"Business Day," 12
*Business Week*, 12

Cable News Network (CNN), 15
   "Business Day," 12
   "Moneyline," 12
Capacity utilization, 6
Cash crunches, 118–147
   assets, holding on to, 119
   college account, withdrawing funds from, 120
   events causing, examples of, 118
   guidelines to follow during, 119
   house, holding on to your, 120
   loans, getting, 120–143
   nonessentials, stopping purchases of, 119–120
Cash or cash equivalents:
   faltering economy, effect of, 57

Cash or cash equivalents (Cont.)
  insuring your cash, 168–169
  interest rates, rise in, 49
  international cash mutual fund,
    buying shares in, 45
  recovering economy, effect of, 55
  war, effect of, 52
CDs: *See* Certificates of deposit (CDs)
Certificates of deposit (CDs), 28–29,
  36
  definition, 36
  interest rates, 28–29, 45, 49
  where to buy, 37
Chapter 7 bankruptcy, 146
Chapter 13 bankruptcy, 146
Clothing, buying at bargain prices,
  175–180
  mail, shopping by, 178–179
  outlets, 175–178
CNN: *See* Cable News Network
  (CNN)
Collectibles:
  faltering economy, effect of, 56–57
  holding on to, 44, 51–52
  interest rates, 44, 48
  recovering economy, effect on, 54
  war, effect of, 51–52
College education, financing, 139–144
  commercial loans for college
    students, 143
  EE savings bonds, 143
  financial aid, 140–142
    federal aid, types of, 141
    PLUS (Parent Loans to Under-
      graduate Students), 141
    SLS (Supplemental Loan to
      Students), 141
    Stafford Loan, 141
Commerce Department reports, 8
Common stock, 19
Community Home Improvement
  Loan, 41
Consumer debts, replacing with home
  equity loans, 20
Consumer loans, 126–128, 140
Consumer price index (CPI), 6–7, 10
  inflation, 7
  recovering economy, effect of, 54
Consumer sentiment, 7

Contracts:
  employment contracts, 100–101
Corporate bonds, 69
Cost of living index, 6–7
CPI: *See* Consumer price index (CPI)
Credit cards, 144–147
  charges, 18, 20, 86
  counseling, 146–147
  loans, 127, 130, 144–145
  low-rate credit cards, getting, 168
  rebuilding your credit, 145
  secured credit cards, 127–128, 145
Creditors, sending "good faith"
  checks to, 86
Credit unions, 32–33, 121
Cutting costs, 163–188

Dining out for less, 170–172
Dividend Reinvestment Plan (DRIP),
  19
Dividends, stock: *See* Stocks
*Donoghue's Money Letter*, 31
*Dow Theory Letters*, 54
DRIP: *See* Dividend Reinvestment
  Plan (DRIP)

*Early Warning Wire*, 27
Economy:
  faltering, what to do, 55–57
  monitoring, 40
  recovery of, what to do if, 53–55
EE savings bonds, 36
  college education, financing, 143
Employee benefits:
  employee stock ownership plan
    (ESOP), 19
  health insurance, 88–89
  retirement plans, 18, 85, 105–107
    withdrawing funds from retire-
      ment savings, 131–132
  severance benefits, 84–85, 107
Employee stock ownership plan
  (ESOP), 19
Employment:
  cities to explore for, 103–105
  contracts, employment, 100–101
  consultant, becoming a, 102
  cutbacks, 73
  executive recruiters, 98

Employment (Cont.)
  fears of losing, 74–75
  finding employment, 91–117
    agencies, 98
    cities to explore, list of, 103–105
    cover letters, 97
    direct contact with companies, 97–98
    executive recruiters, 98
    fields with potential for, 101
    fields lacking potential for, 101–102
    40-Plus Clubs, 97
    interview hints, 99–100
    job strengths, worksheet for identifying your, 93
    morale, keeping up your, 99
    networking, 94–96
    New York Times, employment section in, 98
    older workers, 105–110
    outplacements, 92, 96–97
    recognizing your talents, 91–92
    rejection letters, answering, 98
    resumés, 94, 97, 98
    want ads, answering, 98
  40-Plus Clubs, 97
  free-lancing, 102–103
  interview hints, 99–100
  moonlighting, 102
  National Association for Self-Employed (NASE), 110, 168
  networking, 94–96
  older workers
    early retirement, 106
    finding work, 107–110
    Older Workers Benefit Protection Act, 107
    Social Security benefits, 109–110
    tips for, 105–110
  resumé, putting together a, 94
  safeguarding your job, things to do, 75
  starting a business, 110–117
    before you begin, things to do, 110–111
    capital, raising, 112–115
    hobby, turning into a business, 111–112
    loans, getting, 113–115
    partner, finding a, 115
    Small Business Administration (SBA), 114–115
    small business owner, pluses for being, 111
    state programs providing assistance for, 116–117
    venture capitalists as source of funding, 115–116
  temping, 102
  see also Employee benefits; Unemployment
Energy and utility bonds, 68–72
Energy conservation, 148–158
  air-conditioner, 154–155
  car, maintaining your, 158
  checklist, 149–151
  electricity, conserving, 153–155
  gasoline, conserving, 157–158
  grant for paying heating and utility, 157
  heat, ways to conserve, 149, 152–153
  Home Energy Assistance Program (HEAP), 157
  oil prices, 159
  recommended energy stocks, 159–162
  refrigerators, maintaining your, 155–156
  stocks, recommended energy, 159–162
  things to do, 149–158
  transportation costs, ways to cut back on, 158
  water, conserving, 154
Entertainment, cutting costs on, 169–170
Envelope system, setting up, 20
ESOP: See Employee stock ownership plan (ESOP)
Expanding economy, what to do, 53–55
Expenses:
  cutting costs, 163–188
  eliminating expenses, 20
  Taxes
    office expenses, deductibility, 173

Expenses (Cont.)
  job-hunting expense, deductibility from taxable income, 87
  *see also* Budgets

Faltering economy, what to do, 55–57
Fannie Mae: *See* Federal National Mortgage Association (Fannie Mae)
FDIC: *See* Federal Deposit Insurance Corporation (FDIC)
Federal Deposit Insurance Corporation (FDIC), 168–169
Federal National Mortgage Association (Fannie Mae), 41, 42
Financial evaluations, obtaining:
  banks, of, 29
  savings and loans, of, 29
Financial News Network (FNN), 15
Financial services, no-fee or discounted, 20
FNN: *See* Financial News, Network (FNN)
Food, cutting expenses on, 172
Foreclosures, 138–139
  foreclosed properties, 41
401(k) plans, 85
  withdrawing funds from, 124, 131

Gasoline:
  conserving, 157–158
  shortages, 50
GNP: *See* Gross National Product (GNP)
Gold, investing in, 44–45, 48–49
  bullion bars, 46
  bullion coins, types of, 46
  deflationary, deepening recession as, 57
  faltering economy, effect of, 57
  gold stocks, 46
  how to buy, 46–47
  inflation, gold as hedge against, 45, 57
  interest rates, rise in, 48–49
  mutual funds, participating in gold through, 46
  recovering economy, effect on, 54

war, effect of, 52
  where to buy, 46
Golding, Jay, 27–28
"Good faith" checks, sending creditors, 86
Greenspan, Alan, 3
Gross National Product (GNP)
  constant or real dollar GNP, 7
  definition, 2, 7
  inflation, adjusting figures for, 7
  real or constant dollar GNP, 7

Health insurance, 88–89
  continuation coverage, 88
  National Insurance Consumers Organization (NICO), tips for maintaining coverage, 89
  unemployed, maintaining coverage when, 88–89
HEAP: *See* Home Energy Assistance Program (HEAP)
Home centers, shopping at as a way of cutting costs, 175
Home Energy Assistance Program (HEAP), 157
Home equity loans, 124, 128, 132–135
  closed-end loan, 133
  costs of, 134
  definition, 133
  line of credit, 133
  replacing consumer debts with, 20
Housing starts, 8
  mortgage rates, sensitivity to, 8
Houston, 104

Indianapolis, 103–104
Individual retirement accounts (IRAs), 86, 87
  withdrawing funds from, 131–132
Industries:
  thriving industries, spotting, 58–72
  *Value Line Investment Survey*, list of industries in, 59
  *see also* Recession-resistant industries
Inflation, 3
  consumer price index (CPI), 7
  factors causing, 3

Inflation (Cont.)
  gold as hedge against, 45, 57
  Gross National Product (GNP),
    adjusting figures of, 7
Insurance:
  cash value, 123
  Federal Deposit Insurance Corpo-
    ration, (FDIC), 168–169
  health insurance, 88–89
  life insurance
    cash value, 123
    loans, 124, 129
  Savings Association Insurance
    Fund (SAIF), 32
  travel insurance, 182
  unemployment insurance, 87, 89–91
Interest rates, 3, 9–10
  affect, 9
  bonds, 35, 43–44, 45, 56
  cash or cash equivalents, 49
  certificates of deposit (CDs),
    28–29, 45, 49
  collectibles, 44, 48
  falling interest rates, 40–47
  gold, 48–49
  investments to make when rise or
    fall in, 10
  loans: See Loans
  money market accounts, 44, 47, 49
  prime rate, 10
  rise in, what to do, 47–49
  stocks, 42, 47–48
  what to do if rise in, 29
Investments, 27–57
  cash or cash equivalents, 45, 49
    international cash mutual fund,
      buying shares in, 45
  certificates of deposit (CDs),
    28–29, 36
  choices for, 36–38
  collectibles, 44, 48
  real estate, 40–42
  safe investments, 28
  U.S. Treasury issues, 31–32
  war, effect of, 49–52
  see also Interest rates; Recession-
    resistant industries; Savings and
    savings plans; types of investments
Iraq, 49

IRAs: See Individual retirement
  accounts (IRAs)

Japan, 49, 57
Jobs: See Employment;
  Unemployment

Leading economic indicators, index
  of, 8–9
Life insurance:
  cash value, 123
  loans, 124, 129
Loans:
  adjustable rate loans, 121, 122
  alternatives to, 120–121
  annual percentage rate (APR), 122
  auto loans, 124, 128
  balloon payment, 123
  brokerage loans, 129–130
  buydown, 123
  cash value, 123
  check overdrafts, 124, 126
  Community Home Improvement
    Loan, 41
  consumer loans, 126–128, 140
  credit card loans, 127, 130,
    144–145
  credit unions, 121
  college education, financing:
    See College education, financing
  family and friends, borrowing from
    130–131
  fees, negotiating, 122
  friends and family, borrowing,
    from, 130–131
  interest rates, 120–131
    adjustable rate loans, 121, 122
    annual percentage rate (APR),
      122
    cap defined, 123
    index defined, 123
    interest defined, 123
    margin loans, 124
    monitoring, 121
    negotiating, 122
  life insurance loans, 124, 129
  obtaining loans to make it through
    recession, 120–139
  rejections, 122

Loans (Cont.)
points defined, 123
prime rate, 123
principal defined, 143
real estate laons, 128–129
rejections, 122
retirement savings, 131–132
secured credit cards, 127–128, 145
secured personal loans, 121, 124, 126
selecting a lender, 120
showing up prepared when applying for, 122
Small Business Administration (SBA), 114–115
smart ways to borrow, 120–125
starting a business, getting loans for, 113–115
terms to understand before borrowing, 122–123
unsecured personal loans, 121, 126–127
ways to borrow, 120–125
see also Home equity loans; Mortgages

Mack, Consuelo, 14
Media coverage, 12–16
Middle East, 49
Minneapolis, 103
Mirabella, Grace, 74
"Moneyline," 12
Money market accounts, 18, 36, 42, 44, 45
Money market mutual funds, 29–31, 45
blue-chip stock, switching to, 54
definition, 29
Monitoring economic situation, 40
Mortgages, 40–42, 135–139
adjustable rate mortgages (ARMs), 135–136
conversion clause, 123
interest rates, 136
assumability, 123
equity defined, 123
falling interest rates, 40
Federal National Mortgage Association (Fannie Mae), 41, 42

fixed-rate mortgages, 136
foreclosures, 138–139
housing starts sensitive to mortgage rates, 8
lowest-rate mortgage, finding, 42
mortgage rates, housing starts sensitive to, 8
refinancing, 137–138
secondary mortgages, 124, 128–129
severance pay being used to pay off, 85
Mutual funds, 38
blue-chip mutual funds, 54
definition, 38
Donoghue's Money Letter, 31
gold, mutual funds as a way of participating in, 46
No-fee mutual funds, 20–21

NASE: See National Association for the Self-Employed (NASE)
National Association for the Self-Employed (NASE), 110, 168
National Credit Union Share Insurance Fund, 33
New York Stock Exchange, 34, 65, 69
New York Times:
"credit market" column in, 9
employment section in, 98
"Nightly Business Report, The" 12, 14–15

Oil companies, list of, 70–71
Oil:
conserving, 149
prices, 159
shortages, 50
Older Workers Benefit Protection Act, 107
Outplacements, 84, 92, 96–97

PBS: See Public Broadcasting System (PBS)
Pension plans: See Retirement plans
Personal finances, taking control of your, 16–17
Portland, Oregon, 104

PPI: *See* Producer price index (PPI)
Producer price index (PPI), 10
Profit-sharing plan, 19
Publications, list of, 16
Public Broadcasting System (PBS)
  "Adam Smith's Money World,"
    12, 13
  "Nightly Business Reporting,
    The," 12, 14–15
  "Wall Street Week," 12, 13–14

Real estate, 40–42
  appraisals, obtaining, 41
  auctions, 41
  Community Home Improvement
    Loan, 41
  equity defined, 123
  faltering economy, what to do,
    55–56
  Federal National Mortgage
    Association (Fannie Mae), 41,
    42
  financing your home, 135–139
  foreclosures, 138–139
    foreclosed properties, 41
  improvements to your home as a
    way of cutting costs, making,
    172–174
  interest rates, 47
  lease-option agreements, 137
  loans, 128–129
  mortgages, 40–42, 135–139
    secondary mortgages, 128–129
  prices, 8
  repossessed properties, obtaining
    list of, 41
  residential auction, 41
  Resolution Trust Corporation
    (RTC), 41
  rise in prices with recovery of
    economy, 53
  selling your home, 53
  unknown area, buying, 41
  war, effect of, 50
Recession:
  beginning of, 2, 8
  budgets: *See* Budgets
  capacity utilization, 6
  consumer price index (CPI), 6–7

Consumer sentiment, 7
cutting costs, 163–188
definition, 2
faltering economy, effect of, 55–57
Gross National Product (GNP), 7
housing starts, 8
impact of, steps to take to ease, 26
interest rates, 9–10
leading economic indicators, index
  of, 8–9
length of, 5
previous recession, 4
  positive characteristics, 5
  unemployment, 11–12
producer price index (PPI), 10
real estate: *See* Real estate
recovering economy, effect of,
  53–55
retail sales, 10
Standard & Poor's (S&P) 500
  index, 10–11
steps to take to ease impact of, 26
terms, interpreting, 5–12
*see also* Interest rates; Investments;
  Loans; Real estate;
  Recession-resistant
  industries; *specific headings*
Recession-resistant industries:
  Abbott Laboratories, 60
  Albertson's, 61
  alcoholic and nonalcoholic
    beverages, 59
  Amoco, 70
  Atlantic Richfield, 70, 160
  "baby bell" companies, 65
  *Barron's*,
  Bell Telephone of Pennsylvania, 71
  blue-chip stocks, list of, 60–64
  bonds, 68–72
  Bristol-Myers Squibb, 61
  categories, of, 59–60
  Chevron, 70
  Coca-Cola, 61
  Colgate-Palmolive, 62
  Consolidated Edison Company of
    New York, 71
  corporate bonds, 69
  debt, companies with little, 67
  definition, 59

Recession-resistant industries (Cont.)
  dividend payers, buying stocks of
    companies having history as
    steady, 66
  drugs, 59
  Duke Power, 72
  electric and gas, 60, 70
  energy and utility bonds, 71–72
  gas and electric, 60, 70
  health care, 59
  Heinz, 62
  high-yielding utility stocks, 68
  household products, 59–60
  Kellogg, 62
  medical supplies, 59
  Mobil, 70
  oil companies, 70–71
  Pacific Gas & Electric, 72
  Pacific Telephone & Telegraph, 71
  Pepsico, 63
  Proctor & Gamble, 63
  Public Service Electric & Gas Co.,
    72
  Ralston Purina, 63–64
  steady dividend payers, buying
    stocks of companies having
    history as, 66
  stocks, 60–68
  Sysco, 64
  telephone and telecommunications,
    60, 71
  Texaco, 71
  Treasury bonds, 69
  utilities, 60
  utility bonds, energy and, 71–72
  utility stocks, high-yielding, 68
  waste disposal, 60
  Waste Management, 64
Resolution Trust Corporation (RTC),
  41
Retail sales, 10
Retirement plans, 19, 85, 87, 106
  early retirement, 106
  401(k) plans, 85
    withdrawing funds from, 124, 131
  Individual retirement accounts
    (IRAs), 86, 87
    withdrawing funds from,
      131–132

  taxation, 85, 87
  vested defined, 123
  withdrawing funds from retirement
    savings, 124, 131–132
RTC: *See* Resolution Trust
  Corporation (RTC)
Rukeyser, Louis, 13–14
Russell, Richard, 54

SAIF: *See* Savings Association
  Insurance Fund (SAIF)
Savings and Loans (S&L), 29
  financial evaluation of, obtaining,
    29
Savings and savings plans, 16–26
  automatic, using, 18
  bonds, purchasing, 18
  credit card charges, 18, 20
  discount brokers, 20, 166
  emergency savings, 27
  employee stock ownership plan
    (ESOP), 19
  envelope system, setting up, 20
  establishing, 17
  expenses, eliminating, 20
  financial services, no-fee or
    discounted, 20
  high rate debts, consolidating, 20
  home equity loans, replacing
    consumer debts with, 20
  money market accounts, 18
  mutual funds, no-fee, 20
  psychology of saving, 2–22
  retirement plans, 19
    withdrawing funds from
      retirement savings, 131–132
  savings account, 32
  stock, 19
  taxes
    deferring, 18
    withholding, increasing, 20
  ways to save, 17, 163–188
Savings Association Insurance Fund
  (SAIF), 32
S&L: *See* Savings and Loans (S&L)
Secured personal loans, 121, 124,
  126
SBA: *See* Small Business Administration (SBA)

Severance pay, 84–85, 107
  mortgage, using to pay off, 85
  taxability, 85
Small Business Administration
  (SBA), 114–115
Smith, Adam, 13, 14
Social Security benefits, 109
S&P: *See* Standard & Poor's (S&P)
  500 index
Standard & Poor's (S&P) 500 index,
  10–11
Stockbrokers:
  commissions of, paying, 20
  discount stockbrokers, 20–21, 166
  list of, 166
Stocks, 28, 33–34, 38, 42
  aerospace, shares of, 51
  American Stock Exchange, 34
  Arkla Inc, 159
  Atlantic Richfield, 70, 160
  Baker Hughes, 160
  blue-chip stocks, 33, 54
    list of, 60–64
    switching money market funds
      to, 54
  capital appreciation, determination
    by market, 33
  certificates of, issuing, 39
  Chevron Corp., 70, 160
  common stock, 19
  conservative stocks, 56
  Consolidated Natural Gas, 161
  definition, 33, 38
  determining price of, 34
  dividends, 34
    Dividend Reinvestment Plan
      (DRIP), 19
    paying out, 34
    reinvesting, 19, 34
  employee stock ownership plan
    (ESOP), 19
  energy stocks, 51, 159–162
  Exxon Corp., 161
  faltering economy, what to do, 56
  financial services, no-fee or
    discounted, 20
  gold stocks, 46
  growth stocks, 34, 56
  Halliburton, 161

improvement in stock prices with
  recovery of economy, 53
income stocks, 34
initial public offering (IPO), 33
interest rates, 42, 47–48
investments: *See* Investments
listed stocks, 34
money market funds, switching to
  blue chip stock, 54
mutual funds, no fee, 20–21
New York Stock Exchange, 34
Phillips Petroleum, 161–162
profit, making, 34
profit-sharing plan, 19
quality growth stocks, 56
Schlumberger, 162
"sector" fund, 51
selling to public, steps for, 33
symbols for, identifying, 40
Texaco, 71, 162
war, effect of, 50–51
*see also* Recession-resistant
  industries; Stockbrokers

Taxes:
  deferring, 18
  home being used as office, 172–173
  job-hunting expenses, 87
  office expenses, deductibility, 173
  points, deductibility, 123
  retirement plans, 85, 87
  severance pay, taxability of, 85
  unemployment compensation, 91
  withholding, increasing, 20
Travel and vacation, saving on,
  180–188
  ads, clipping, 184
  airfares, 184–186
  children, taking them on business
    trips, 187–188
  company discounts, 181
  courier, becoming a, 180–181
  cruises, 187
  discounts, how to get, 180–183
  farm and ranch family vacations,
    188
  foreign currencies, exchange rates,
    183
  hotel bills, 186

Travel and vacation, saving on (Cont.)
    insuring your trip, 182
    last-minute travel club, joining, 182
    senior citizens, discounts for,
        181–182
    summer camps, 188
    swapping homes, 188
    traveler's checks, shopping for, 186
    *Travel Smart*, 186
Treasury bills, 10, 31, 36, 49
Treasury bonds, 31, 36, 69
Treasury notes, 31, 36

Unemployment, 11–12, 73–118
    budgeting yourself when
        unemployed, 84–87
    cutbacks, 73
    dealing with the shock of being
        unemployed, 75–84
        children, explaining to your,
            81–82
        family, help from, 80
        recession blues, coping with,
            82–83
        recognizing your feelings, 78
        stages of recovery, 79
    "downsizing," 73
    family, help from in dealing with
        being unemployed, 80
    finances, taking care of your, 84–87
    fired, getting, 73, 75–77
        guidelines to follow if fired,
            76–79
        positive aspects, 79–80
        40–Plus Clubs, 97
    "good faith" checks, sending
        creditors, 86
    health insurance, 88–89
    high, when, 7
    job-hunting expenses, deductibility
        from taxable income, 87
    layoffs, 75
    maximizing your income, 86–87
    outplacements, 84, 92, 96–97
    recession blues, coping with, 82–83

    retirement plans, 85
    severance pay, 84–85
    "streamlining," 73
    unemployment insurance, taking,
        87, 89–91
    warning signals at work place,
        74–75
    *see also* Employment
U.S. Treasury issues, 31–32
    forms of, 31
    interest rates, 42
    Treasury bills, 10, 31, 36, 49
    Treasury bonds, 31, 36, 69
    Treasury notes, 31, 36
Unsecured loans, 121, 126–127
Utility bonds, energy and, 68–72
Utility stocks, companies with
    high-yielding, 68

Vacations, saving on: See Travel and
    vacations, saving on

*Wall Street Journal*, 12, 29
"Wall Street Journal Report, The,"
    14
"Wall Street Week," 12, 13–14
War, effect of
    bonds, on, 51
    cash or cash equivalents, effect on,
        52
    collectibles, on, 51–52
    declaration of war, what to do if,
        49–52
    gasoline shortages, 50
    gold, on, 52
    industrial areas, 50
    investments, on, 49–52
    oil shortages, 50
    possible situations causing severe
        economic changes, 50
    real estate, on, 50
    stocks, on, 50–51
Warehouses, shopping at as a way of
    cutting costs, 179–180
Western Europe, 50, 57